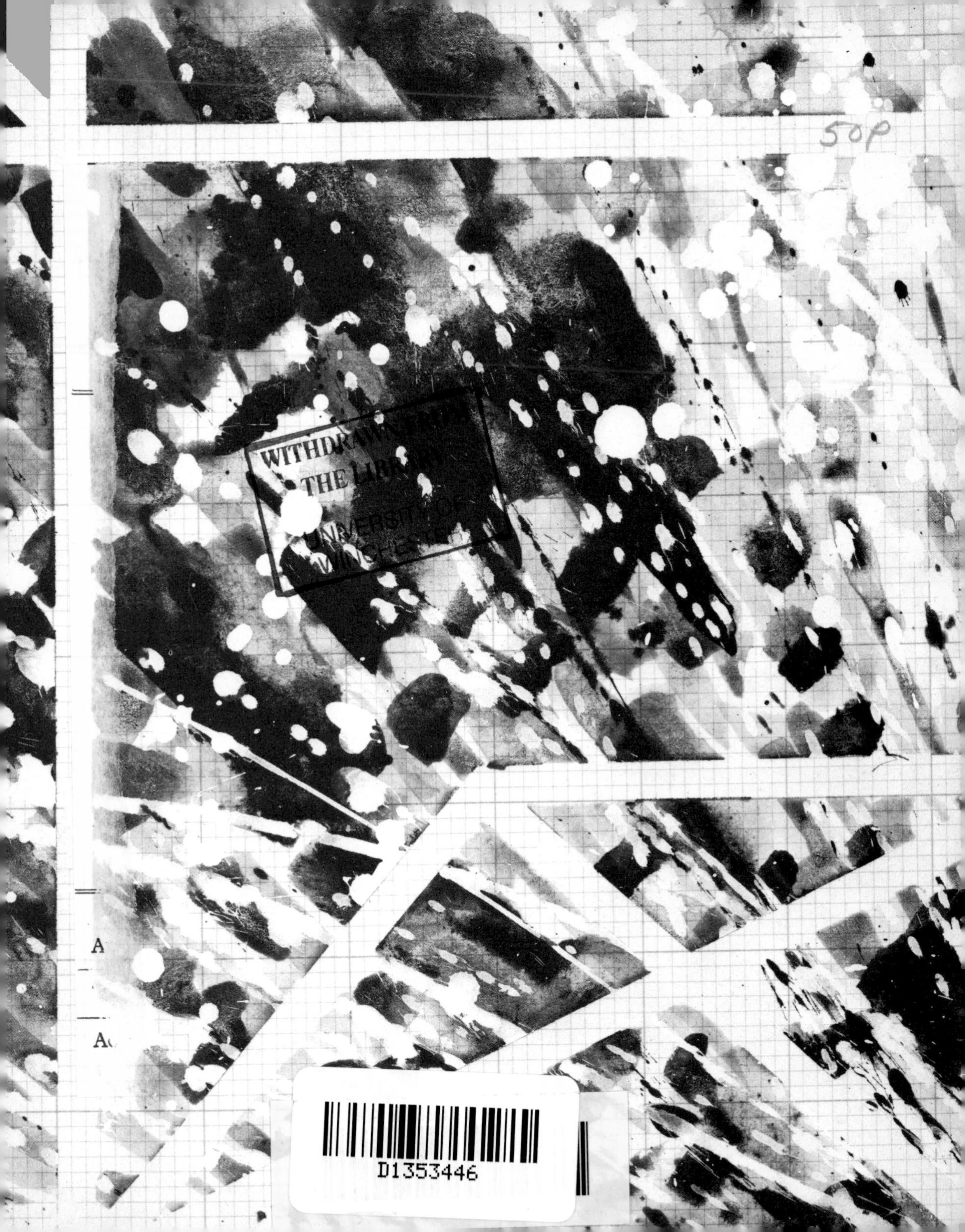

50p

The Wolverhampton Wanderer. Peter Blake.

MICHAEL HOROVITZ

The Wolverhampton Wanderer

AN EPIC OF BRITANNIA

In Twelve Books
With a Resurrection & a Life

for Poetry United

with illustrations by

Peter Blake, Michael Bloom, Jeff Cloves, Mal Dean, R. Elson, P. G. Findlay, Michael Foreman, Mike Francis, John Furnival, Bob Godfrey, Jeff Goldner, Richard Hamilton, Adrian Henri, David Hockney, Marigold Hodgkinson, Pete Hoida, Michael Horovitz, Patrick Hughes, Mike McInnerney, Paul Kaplan, Pete Morgan, Stephen Morris, Gabi Nasemann, Jeff Nuttall, David Oxtoby, Tom Phillips, Adam Ritchie, Nick Roberts, Ron Sandford, Colin Self, Shepard Sherbell, Feliks Topolski, Michael Tyzack.

LATIMER, London

4 5 7

Publication details

The complete poem first published 1971
by Latimer New Dimensions Limited, 4 Alwyne Villas, London N1 2HQ

Paperback SBN 901539 14 7
Hardback SBN 901539 15 5
Signed & limited edition SBN 901539 16 3

This book has been designed by Michael Horovitz, tempered by John L. Smith, set by Mason & Weldon Ltd on an IBM Selectric Composer, paper supplied by P.F. Bingham Ltd, covers and jackets printed by Chase Printers Ltd, and printed & bound by Latimer Trend & Co Ltd, Whitstable, England.

Contents

The quotations at Half-Time are from *Hunger* by Rimbaud, and the Old English elegies *The Seafarer* and *The Wanderer*

Of this first edition, 100 copies have been numbered and signed by the author and the artists and photographers who have contributed to the book.

Illustrations

Acknowledgements

The author extends his heartfelt thanks to all these artists and photographers, with apologies to those whose identity he was unable to trace; and also to Elly Beintema, Pete Brown, Jan & Benjamin Falkiner, Jean Gow, Mary Harron, Frances Horovitz, Ozzie Jones, Cathy Kiddle, Adam Kops, David MacLagen, Peter Mayer, John Smith, the USIS Picture Library and the Wolverhampton Express & Star, for their help towards the completion of this magnum opus.

And also to the editors and publishers of the following, in which earlier versions of some of the sections have appeared: *Amazing Grace*, *Broadsheet* (Dublin), Warwick University's *Campus*, the Wolverhampton *Express & Star*, *6d Poems* (Whole Press, Guildford), *Rumpus* (Swansea), and the anthology *C'mon Everybody* (Corgi Books); excerpts have also been read by the author on John Peel's *Night Ride*, *Breakthrough* (Radio London), *Alive & Kicking* (London Weekend TV), and at various public venues.

The publisher himself regrets that Jackie Milburn does not appear in this book.

Preface

This is the definitive version of my most ambitious poem-sequence to date, upshot of nearly three years' intricate pruning and extensions since it began on a train, en route for reading at Wolverhampton art school. This first visit to the Midland stronghold, in the autumn of 1968, coincided with that of a Cockney football crowd; which aroused the tranquil recollection of pleasurable emotions experienced whilst playing and watching soccer during childhood and adolescence.

The resonant name of the Wolves and their magnificent 'oldgold & blacksilk' garb (suggestive of medieval lists – 'Clashing hoar-frost joust yestern straddled the weir'), and that of the Arsenal (whose stadium was easiest of access) were my highlights in the native mythology – & endure in the poem as the tribal tension between wilde beestes of Primeval Mercian forests, and the scientific precision of generation upon generation of British Grenadiers – a permanent All-Star London-based artillery of champions.

The **Wanderer** grew and grew – if not as "naturally as the leaves to a tree", at least as inevitably as the patterns of play & dance that spring up around one – to the proportions of a vast animated history painting, from manifold sources I'd nourished over the intervening years. – Above all, probably, from the Ur-origins of poetry in English I'd studied and read aloud at Oxford – **Beowulf** & the Anglo-Saxon Elegies in which – as in the universal linguists Milton, Joyce and Eliot – poetry meant informed *making*, forgeing out a 'new' language. And yet a popular dialect, a spoken language that wells from the middle of society, as it did through "those brave translunary things" of primitive lore – retailing the stories of their peoples & interpreting their gods, usually with musical accompaniment at community celebrations. Thus you may find revived in this book qualities, unlooked for by the neo-classicists, which the Ancients held in common with us today: which the post-renaissance idea of art as a one-man show in a stratified 'book-set' has blurred – that is, art as organic part & parcel of real life (no less real) in our freshly primal audio-visual culture, instantly projected and received via public performance.

The radiation of public poet-meets across North America, Russia & Britain, from bar-rooms and village greens to global bowls, sports arenas and others the size of Mayakovsky Square & Central Park, is common knowledge by now. What has not often been remarked (by intellectuals, at least) is the changed definition & meaning of poetry this incurs. And further, that the nearest many people get to the epic moment & catharsis which used to be provided by Homer and Greek tragedies comes at (open-air) poetry/rock festivals or – more regularly – on those Saturday afternoons & illuminated mid-week evenings when the populace in its *millions* identifies, 'to a man', with the 22 on the field — collective psyche played out and, in the fullness of full-time, resolved (like my poem) in "peace of mind / all passion spent". The tongue that describes this play — each one, for its spectators, the 'match of the day' — instinctively turns to heroic diction, a high-pitched urgency and spontaneous rhetorical involvement — Radio Newsreel our Olympic torchbearer. . .

The arts still only achieve this kind of demotic intensity occasionally, more often by happy accident than design — as happened around the first International Poetry Incarnation at Albert Hall (for Philip French of the New Statesman "my St Crispin's Day/Agincourt moment of the 1960s, the Public occasion of the past ten years one would most have regretted missing"). But this event was only proof, on the grand scale, of what had been demonstrated on these islands since the 'angry decade' — that the poet's voice has no business, these days, to stay choked in the desert. More and more poet-troubadors have been taking their rightful place within the environment as public spokesmen & authentic folk-heroes — at mass gatherings as well as through the media — Dyland Thomas and Bob Dylan; Yevtushenko, who — like his coevals Kerouac and Corso served a useful apprenticeship to 'action poetry' as sports reporter; Ginsberg — who's pointed, by howling his **Kaddishim** the world over, a "redemption from wilderness, way for the wanderer" to so many, reminding them they're *not* alone.

Soccer affords an *available* universe in Britain, a 'free for all' range — allegorical and actual: one of the only major 'worlds' open for anyone — a 'working-class hero' — to conquer, inhabit. The most obvious other is on the boards, as pop-singer, minstrel or bard — transmitting energy in words, music and skilled physical articulation; and it's this curious analogy of troupers — professional footballer and itinerant poet, which is explored in detail on these pages. For my concern is never exclusively with football, as a nice colourful subject, but with synthesis — the invention of a viable, and relevant, midcentury epic.

So it's a large part of my hope & intention that literati, too, will find much to enjoy here at their leisure — to meet again, for instance, the Old English Wanderer and Seafarer — Middle English lyricism — Blakean—Whitmanic Songs of the open Road—runner, who delights in blithe wordmeat — 'the game of life played by foot & ear / muscle & voice & tomorrow's yesteryear' with the whole world looking on; yet probes beneath the glamour, tracking down the veteran on his last legs, bereft of team, mate or "giver of cups and rings". . . My figure of the Wanderer is essentially a man 'of the people', surviving on his stoicism and his craft: scanning each face he meets for warmth and wonderment — or only (in charter'd Smethwick & Wolverhampton) marking the weakness and woe of race-hatred: one who might choose for his epigraph these lines from Scott's **Last Minstrel** of 1805 —

Dejectedly, and low, he bow'd,
And, gazing timid on the crowd,
He seemed to seek in every eye
If they approved his minstrelsy;
And, diffident of present praise,
Somewhat he spoke of former days,
And how old age, and wand'ring long,
Had done his hand and harp some wrong. . .

At best, form is content, and content form. The movements of the work are disposed for the most part in sturdy blank verse – a use of measure akin to that of **Paradise Lost** (& likewise made up of 12 books – but without a rigidly preconceived aim), "the sense variously drawn out" in long breaths from line to line & verse paragraph to verse paragraph. I've deliberately kept the metre flexible throughout – accented, *not* syllabic, i.e. accented & varied *by the reader* – whether subtly in the 'mind's ear' or experimentally out loud: allowing for a wide spectrum of effects – mimetic 'goal lines' – 3-D, not linear-flat on the page; lifted off it with the by-play of Wm Carlos Williams's 'variable foot' into free-form fragmentations (as in the word-sounds of modern black-amerikan blues) punctuated by breath units only, onomatopoeic improvisations, tongue-in-cheek antique & mock-heroic hyperbole – and truly felt Heroics, Laments & symphonic cadences. – Always as befits the matter, style and tone of the several phases the Wanderer passes through, viz – reminiscence, odes, epodes, (jazz) choruses, erotica, 'umbiblica', surreal-real flashes, social-realist narrative, polemica, tragedy, comic relief and epiphany.

– Now read on: the wolves are running – the game is afoot!

M.H. August 1971

Prologues

Left out, long dropped
Out the pace-set starsystem uniform norm
Aries quivers. Restless, wouldbe ever-kicking
Poor player — old dog sits skulking, would be
Hulking brute — to maul out
The life leftover to kill

. . . Licking, picking claphand-blest
Wounds of old. Sits disconsolate, sips —
Lovelaced. . . tea going cold. Glass-cased
Decorations hardly stave off
His old feelings —
Of having been wrongly sold out
Of brawn-brine and masculine Bacchic bout.

He watches TV — no wolves at home's door
Yet longs for. . . he knows not what
. . .He stares — London roundabouts
& swings —
he listens — spouts
— & sweetly sings

— But: to whom? — White sheep
Of wolfbane shorn? — At dawn
Sees — Golden Lads. . . not He —
Gingerly pads his gingerbread cave
— Snuffs at snout soft-snarling —
Rallies and raves . . .rediscovers and waves
The Wóden Wand . . .follows his feet
Through the back of beyond

— Body spurs beyond doubt
Mind turns
round & over
& out

. . .Cricket shirrs through the night
. . .Mothpulse stirs for
"more light —

New day smiles — sun beguiles
Long gone wolfplight . . .some time
Wizard of action
. . .ambition revives:
He shaves no more — packs his basic
Store of lore . . .starts for Stonehenge

. . .from Eros . . .looses glee
just to be —
Off on the open road again
— & will let it grow —
A- wandering go - and blow any place —
No 'foreshone ways seeking, to save his face
But to grow as long and wily and weird
As the broad-grinning beard of —
Almighty Anon.

Find him if you can
. . .the game wolfman
Before, cheered — or booed
to fly on
He's doggone done it
again — really
gone
gone
gone
— Yarnspinner moves on
And stays still
— Moving
— Standing
— Tracking
. . .Deep, chill
. . .Grooving
(as they say, today
— the young, at play. . .

Somewhere out there tossing lank longhair
Woody wolfbines wander chundering on
— Travel, at the glittering gaze
Of man's newly beshotten litter-strewn moon
— Likewise beaming
The cajoleing crowds' monsoon.

— There in the heavy voice-rended air
As here, growl out for their fancy — rare
Sirloin of groin — or fairest, secret
Imagination's feast;
growling out
The kenning best they know
At Great — and Ingrate investors' behest

. . .Doing their multichannel thing
. . .Writing home — and a way
Through each charter'd wrong,
Each right of play
— but will not Belong. . .

Crowded oft with new home teams
— Weighed Word's worth, alone —

Then with battered seadogs rose again to intone

— Went aflame at the groundlings' microphone
— Hungry willful expectant throng
Barking on their dappled light brigades
To swoorl supercharged, resound the grape gong
— Divining arcane
Naked wordspread — insane!
. . .Treading on
— in loss, tie — or
Winning
— beginning again
— Footballer-poet roadrunning Reader
Tracks atomic, comic
and gnomic strain
That Meadhalls be born again in the plain —

Wolfcity, flocculent footballfane —
My lute awaking — navvy-cradled crane
Changes gear — shifts the clouds
— it's Olympic Year!

— Hear now's massy roar in a ripe-tun'd score
Threading threnodied thralls ahoist paw by paw. . .

England's rage on page rekindles the cry —
Claw-scrive to the core — Oh pitch the Try high!
— Go: 'Load every rift with ore'
— Deny gravity — Yuy! The wing-halves shy
Darting migrant forwards to fly
Over full-backs flipped out
down the hopless skid vat
— Fallen flat at the natty scat-style of bard's boot
That storms swooping forms, flailing far out of reach
Of defensive projections that pompously preach
— Aught else but the valiant variant foot.
— Only grass-eye
to eyeball
Sees how it's made
Fitfully floating the vulpine arcade
— Oldgold and blacksilk punting glade

. . .As ere Rugger, or the Base ball-games beck begat
Their queasy hand-snatch Force titillation
Teeming soccer teams worked sturdy association
Gleaning level returns from their highway code

. . .At the crossroads barrier of Mid-Euston station
Dig a spade — change a mode — move the chessboard to Ode

. . .on out over the hill
'that sweet golden clime' sings
— and its echo rings —
Hark — the Sunflower sings —

Poet — Arise and go now —
Your journey is nearly done
. . .Come alive, and know now —
'Tis **you** are the sainted son —

But Orpheus casts back his tormented eyes
To the city, for pity of his calling
. . . lies
With new squads of schoolboy supporters to scream
"Good ole Wolves"
— gallant high & dried jumbo-giant tureen

. . .Those Wolves, those Wolves
Those wandering Wolves —
Crude-letter'd unfettered 'forerunners

Their fancy footwork
Drove sheepdogs berserk
— And nearly shot up the Gunners:

— Arsenal, Arsenal — sing soaring Savannahs
— Brilliantine-boyhooded banners
    — Singing Arsenal Arsenal
   Give us Another One
    — We are the Arsenal Boys Gorblimey
    — Arsenal Arsenal — Give us Another One —
   We are the Arsenal Boys. . .

— My Team — common dream
Of wartime Limey juniors agleam
— Dream of Me dabfoot amid that accord
— Shining Angel-land's lolloping lord
— Initiation to heaven secured and sooth-sealed
On that final Elysium's ever green yield

— Brimful-filling the Cup, dinning cymbal
& field-metric shield
back-heel'd from Achilles
— Passed through from Aprillés
Samsónic shoures
— Pressing live matches
like fragrant flowers
To survive the mesh of flesh sweat-steamed.

Faith blesses and shapes
Though myth rapes, and desists
To be stitched in chronicle-
coracled oracle
— The stained glass lists
Come brightlight wander-marching
fresh dew silver'd mists
Of Arthur and Odin and Jove's tempest trove
To Ulyssean rovers
— bloat of May Balls over

— We'll wordwade these seizures of stomp-stirr'd acclaim
That rite eft steal the soccersuckt soul

. . .And Those Feet **did** walk,
do talk
— **shall** know:

If I am Footballer, Poem is Goal!

Continuum

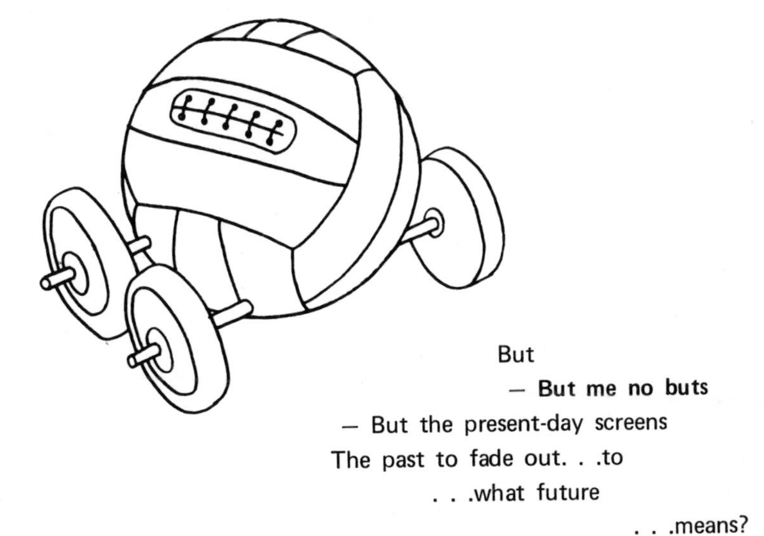

But
— **But me no buts**
— But the present-day screens
The past to fade out. . .to
. . .what future
. . .means?

. . .The scenes have changed
beyond recognition
. . .Abstracts of nuclear fission
forgotten
. . .Overlaid with group sounds 'the'
word blurs
— out of position
. . .What's left
undecayed?
— The sporting tradition?
Leaf fables?
— Magician; —
Stick facts to thy tracts
— the diesel fumes —
the city limits —
the players
have their moments:

Trainees catch the trains — old linesmen abscond
For the love generation stone age frond
Balling blonde on blond open at front and rear
— 3rd Eye — I Ching — it all means some thing. . .

Clashing hoar-frost joust yestern straddled the weir
Winter's windgrips lashed at the outsider's fear

— Now nolonger beware — peace on earth is shared

— Come, dig in
Wolfseer —
Real-life venues with menus replenish the ear
Well earned winnings and takings banish the blear
And we each are the man we always were —

Yeah?

— Then why are **would**-be & "Shall know" still lurking here?

Because: even at Wolve's duff bluff
tough-tighten'd belt
— HEROICS GLINT 'NEATH THE MARSH-MOTTLED PELT
And will out
. . .through seasonal frieze
to melt.

I write
what I like
Hike
or ride
motor-
bike
& — somedays
needs strike —
Mike
to mike,
Poet to public
engineer:

— Moon bound,
Creature tongued —

Jacob's ladder
— Verse- rung'd

. . .Oh Animal Citizen man-to-man field plan
Sailing upright to Mars-shot pyrotechnics steeled
Sport of words locked close, and closer spelled
From the 18th Century to Tuesday Weld

. . .Links chains of gangs — key-bangers of wolves
To recharge dissembling police-state spires
Spark plug resonant ringings of rockface and streams
— Gutburst floodgates — overspill pyres
Twang the break through tight cages
— to **realise** dreams.

Immortals.
And that this should be
But — yes — today
— at the "Sea of Tranquility"
— America — **'tis** Thee i sing
— Lunar Muse
— Solar universe
— Everything —
Love, poetry — undying embers
— remembered
Glow through old age and infirmity

. . .when Erastus played on his ol' kazoo
& Murphy — No, Baby **Dodds** at the skins —
heard see-sawing Sam on the bass viol
. . .Vikings villaged, I flexed my shins —

'The Family' & more — de Bassi Profúndi —
Great Aunt Amadéi did smile
on us tenderfoot star-struck wolf cubs
— getting better — and more — all the while

. . .Like —
those monk-spondeed dizzy spells yardbird still blow —
Portobellow Road gardenlove — play spaces grow
Atop blowtorch Marathon poemjoist snow
— Moonlight white in
to black
& back — Meta-morse rolled
. . .out the barrels, cat-carols — & butter-
bugs flew
. . .fresh cocoons, new axés, found saxaphone filth
— things like
Now I'm Coming, Virginia Woolf

. . .liked what we had, glad we were mad
. . .that we're born,
and made — dared Who's **really** afraid
of the Big and the Bad
& the panto wolf the cop-curs had* —
Oh dad, dear dad — you poor old lad
— If it only was all as easy as thad†

* — See the author's lyric transcription **The Writing on the Walls** (in Alan Bold's anthology of revolutionary poems 'From the Left')

† — as in Thad Jones — blue-skied trumpeter of vintage Count Basie bands

— Trilling songthrush champagne-crush moats of wolf
Avalaunching flying Chaucer-Jazz Age Wolves
— Rabid savage-lunching rockwilled wolves

. . .Covered traces
— outfaced Faces
jibbered — took stands
— & delivered
— high-sounding wolf terms
making flesh
lineamented
Grecian Urns

— Laid me down
From vague Mandalay- me
— Dream'd of Sun
Through Sea

— Woke to Tree
— & sang on
Scree-height
— Chose the angels' fruit —
Wing'd light

— Over pebbled Lake
Danced to Thee
Countless steps
— Sought no fee

. . .Drew in clear light rays,
Filtered nodding oak bays
Sapped in leaves
Of grass, strings and flutes
Of folk
— Woke from yoke
To invoke

Classical viols
And William Bloke

— Clapped out —

caroused on

from doggerel days

— Plucked the cling from ivy's brook bonded peaches

Learned — the craft of Making — with Daedalus faking —

— Skipped to mid-Heaven's marvel

with lambs of Blake

— bands of angels

— for pure goodness' sake

– Middle Earth
– rebirth

Slak'd my thirst
for world's worth

– enliven'd the shelves'
tales of lions and wolves
lying down
with elves

– Turned to
– human beings
– enjoying themselves!

Preludes

. . .Phineas Shenanigan
vied King Hengest O'Flanagan
. . .Heralds high time the hoarser
Ceilidhs began again

. . .And of course in cold season's prick-shrivel clutches
The crotch-happy clothes horses
also ran again

— Yet no tennis courtships
Warm auld glee-riders up a vein

— Oh no: playing footer —
footer it was
Kept us kids
and "the forces"
coming on strong again

— Slain comrades' morale boost
airs zane

. . .on the game again —

Fervent first-footing it
— flushing, blushing
In youthtime 'twas pleasure — summoned early by birds
As if first e'er to breathe any winding morn's wreath
— Knew we flew — Swam, lepped elate o'er the heath
— Grailblazing bee-swarms —
hollow hills paper chaste

— Far and wide across near country running
Our balls new born brains — o'er the east and the west
— Hun-fled on the Wulfrun
— athwart machine- gunning
To POOL BRITTANIA — diverting the rest
Of the flaccid tests of slave-graven learning
— Craven backache of rime-
waste of bodybait yearning
— The land slid to nowhere — desire killed burning
Deadhead leaden-hand lengths — detension's shut gate

— Old-tyme measures — taught hard prison's fate
Kept in late at hook'd line-biting long afterschool
Drilled to absolute ablatives — sorrowing Rule

— No wonder Sapiens barged past each blunder
— Ignored easy bait
— hated nothing but Hate,
Took the Judges' proverbial tools with a pinch
Of mother wit and inchworming hide,
Slung satchels aside pumping air to glide —
Change positions
cut loose
strike- kick
wheel back
To centre, nest
— & coldeyed ride on

— Nary a pause to acknowledge applause
Excepting spirit-exultation
Every man-
jack —
ace-
embracing

— Springs of beau zest
Planted jesterly erst (as of lake lapping swan)
— Thirst of dance
— for that burst
Dam floodgates stilled tension
Nourished fire — rekindled the choir
— Earth-hidden clan
From the deepest iron root- heat of man

. . .Clam of Ram fountain'd best
Sunspot-on
at sport: craft-strait, tackle-taut

. . .Lining up, number'd pup —
Unruffled, tho' scuffled (Charlemagne-brandied
Champions fell muffled
At the black pools' tangerine R-K-O-tune fork'd tower
& lay gall-drenched beach- darkling hour on hour
With Belisha- beacons hotpoint switched on all night
Watching over the bottle-razed Celtic site

— Carcarried Muse-married knobby-kneed goons go on
Out of Marx Brothers Ignu and daisy-pull'd chains
— Flispering Rabbi Burns' lallans-lipp'd lanes
Wolf-weaving wild penelop'd downtrodden skeins
To rise —
heading aside domesticate strains

. . .Hand-in-handing — lyrestranded — then Landroving Bands
Patchwork upsurgeing, merging grass roots and wands
— Transforming the shiv'riest rum bum shots
To scorchers —
parch'd panfalls of apple bombardment —
Wordscrum in mind-sight clearset to sheer beauty

. . .Harp- limbering, pawsprung rhythm heaving –
Wandering minstrel priest believing
His feet
speed
speech –

Knowledg'd
— so much to teach —
Now rarely grieving
The man-ball
— root
— Tall Tree of Life
unleaveing

— So he save —
The Golden Grove —
Felt fleece
& fulsome fresh fruit thereof.

Moving finger —
Open my craze, to tell true

. . .About you, long-ear'd setter — so delicate set
In all ways of your justly wandering sight

. . .Steer the dark night
and float
On iceberg'd capacity —
Your sportive nature's
Actual audacity
— in despite of
City — Vanity
— Jerking on
— Self
— as Boss —
Play rather
the Phoenix —
Father Hopkins, or
Los
Wearing out both hands
at Jerusalem's furnace

— sifting sands
in wonder- whirling
the mace. . .

Grace uplifts
from the wrack
of dead bard's bright face –

Canny crow's nest Mariner
– tho breast beaten
She – White Goddess stoppeth
– One sure goal in three

– He's bent scrambling to fly
So spry o'er the tree
– Might never collect
Any regular fee

– She pales
His dark clusters
To full moon's lustre-
lucent majesty.

As night follows day
Light succeeds
"mental fight –

So. . . acknowledge, and show –
Just as we throw
Snowball strength at play,
Wrought vessels from clay

. . .So live
– and give it all away –

What we know
– All we lovingly do.

— Shows . . .when you do get going
You've ignored the publicity

— But sealy agility
Squirms back — eels
— to servility:

Vultures wait to slay
Their proper prey
— Who walks too blithe
Some "own" snail-slithy way
. . .Every time you split
human
atoms
to score
— you're rejoin'd
by the coin
of the realm
for more
— Hail Hosannah-hurrah
Of questmates and squaw.

"Don't question: blow blind. **Never** mind" — some say —
"It's all a 'mind trip'. . . You're hip — Trouper: play —
"Swing with numbers and rhyme,
till the timeless of time
"Move on — or stay with it — snow blooms on the privet. . .
"Your heart-song can't go wrong — as long as you live it"

— I'm not so sure. I like
The general idea. . .
But the general idea
Must needs abjure. With the particular Wanderer —
Wax and wane.
Alert — to the stars — in the rain. . .

Without message, pure
. . .He hopes

— the old whore.

SHED SHED SHED SHED
SHED SHED YOUR INHIBITIONS, BOYS
IN WHICH THE POET, LEFT FOR DEAD, FINALLY BEGINS TO PRACTICE WHAT HE PREACHES!

Grope

SING – Swing on sing play
Up Sing Oyez Olé
 – On the ball, ton-up tall
Frenzied feet of clay

Make way, make hay
For the slithering beast to be

– For the beast will out –
Dog on earth – run free

. . .Who'ld blunt-bind desires but puts off the day
His own wolfhooded nature wins real free play. . .

Sing O Yea – sweet spindle-bum Lady stay
– Shed kinky-boot laces and Ho Nonny Nays
– Stripped to the fur let's play all the ways
We know: Gaunt Venus – Mount! Oh Cupidinous Lure

. . .Dare-bedevilled 'ERECTION – DEVELOPMENT –
DEMOLITION'
. . .Hear Now – Reconstruction: Animole Mission

. . .Yoho Let's Go – panting Wanderlust –
Raven bellicose past Zooland's paltry tossed crust
That daren't trust India, China
– 3rd and 4th worlds away
Cussed out by the nation-states warring for pay

– Holla there Wanderer, unclench thy mail'd fist –
Here's unquenchable jolly miller's grist
For ground for wolf for shaft to be kissed
And suckled and stiffen'd at well-temper'd tryst
Together in communal settlement's hay

– For tender fang beneath the skin to foray
And withal redound fecund buck-roundelay.

* – i.e., for the Body of the Work: unto Bestial Rock- Bottom)

Deep spirit-fuck,
within hoof-hunt's hallowed bounds
Of space for boundless leap chalk'd out
with oaks asurf the Druid turf

. . .Tho "realist" bloodhounds
Contest that turf, and pointers
Close in – to smelt the heat
Of Limehouse Blues that paint the street
Chasing freemasons' space at gangbang's mauve wharf
– The little people outlive it all

– Hand over the ball
& word of your pass
To the dwarf at the gate
– & pass, and laugh:
Join the dance – take your chance
– "All the world" looking on
– Re- make it – accrue,
Turning swink's existential screw

– Turning on – overturning it
over askew
And on – each and every – lovely you
– Footballman –
& to Thee – Aphrodite
– yet more nubile without
your Kayser-Bondor nightie

– Swithen & fondled, fuss'd over & fanned
On the once – *twice*-a-week grand
all-afternoon stand

. . .An' somewheres behind stairs your foreplay gets canned
For the garland-bored chairman's windowbox gland
—His internal circuit hoards frames they'd have banned
(Shots the F. A. watch committees can't understand)
– The hanging carrot, special bonus – earth-frothmother spann'd
Bosom catchments lower'd – so that nosegay wolf swerves
Sniffing bouquets huge rise 'neath Chianti-bask'd curves
– The size of prize footballs! –

Hildegard Volmering, 18. She let six through, but her ten brothers put up a terrific fight.

pete
Morgan

— Those fullblown charms
Into place poise the footman, unnerve him to arms,
Dandle hands that might finger — but granted
The signal — to linger, svelte swinger
— To stretch out, touch and tamper — nibble nipple, no sin
Coming down in bare skin to slip the thing in

— Squeeze lush bubbling boobs, squelch her hilt of hot hole
In and out, steady treadle to slow or fast bowl —
Playmate-mistress unveiling volcanic goal
She lies, legs up, guiding eyes
— Twitching toes — twinkling, winking —
"I can see you and I know what you're thinking"
Lolls — made up to the mini-mark perfect fit — yet
Bodes dismay to the playboy who assumes This is It

. . .For She Caesar's is, reserving her toll
. . .Doll of destruction — swaddles her roll
. . .Jockeys none but the championship-winning foal —

Circe's sceptre tricks — flaunts nectar, but licks
— Calamity astride
the hide of her victim. Feeds her own
Avaricious appetite only — dangles pussy for cream —
Oozes her physick of gym-slip'ry kicks
— Then swivels & mocks the pink positing pricks*

And collects, on another advance
Another pools-founded fortune ejects;
Sticks out for top triplicate-drawer'd fee,
Bleeds unmoved a cut clot — thudding heart, ailing knee
And plays on at her game — men are all the same
— Thinks nothing of passing on pox at a toss
Of her crinoline-lacquer'd kittykempt locks:

— It's a nice game
milking cocks, she crows
In caviar comfort, slides through fashion shows
Where she poses hose —
And whisks away priceless gowns scot-free

* — The perhaps untoward length of these misogynistic lines is on the ground of groping to be Alexandrine, Hexapodes (i.e. six-footed 'heavies').

Having served to tease and tempt — to tickly entrance
The romp-ruptur'd Capstain's tiller to dance
His Vitals away for the Cup
and a tup
— super-succulent sup
Or minutest position shift — divisional advance
— Glist'ning good of the Club, bellyrub at the hub
Of good press to pared breast at the lips of promotion
— Jogg'd on by the hubbub
— massive milling commotion —
Every man-jack crushed with him — close-packed tourneytub
— Swaying fervent fleets flayed on a treacherous ocean
Come together, come through —
spent sport's buttonhole nub
Yells from bellowing results-sheet — long the losers blub
— 'wrc
& no doubt
but fresh fligh
Rubs out word's prong

— But the chillblain'd rosetted childers cry Fie
And commuters sigh
— humble dues — to Thee,
Gleeman's cosmic all-knowing Eye
Under clothcap diggers' well-versed protection
— Beats reflex, kicks wrench to resurrection,
Hits left halves of bitter pulsating anew
To shoe poesy's firm fastness, run recklessly through
The grunty- grouped punter-poop'd Philistine crew

Tho groupies at grope fear no Puritan Pope
— Like Delilah, Bathsheba — soften the soap,
Midcentury Davids through word-slings elope
Penning psalms that release us from Babel's tight alms
To farms and free ales and flitch without bitch
At the spaces of Erin, West Ham and Shoreditch
But the Bible and Ossian and Swedenborg's itch
Behind them
— Loud-hailer halloo highest white
from scarr'd pitch —

Wandering Jew on Joycean spree
Ball-bearing all pall to tapestry glee

. . .Spurts of sun filter red o'er the guilder'd greens' leaves

Laid Out to the eaves

from the centre spot

There on the floodlit loom of grass

Outflitting fireflies — spearless teapee

Of Hiawatha's

— new age troubadors' way –

Thus all wanders

— eventually

Make home, hit hay —

Get there —

lay

. . .Scores settled pools spumed cups netted

— UNbound —

Byrnieless brassieres loosed to the mound

— Fond intertwin'd rapture — human paradise found

i' the green with your mate — & without, all passions unwound

— in busty ars longa — in shorts,

played out in the round

— PARADISE NOW — regain'd — new found

— Round house-forts — molden treasuries

await — a new Pound

— Go to, hungry hound!

—Snake your squall

— make your sound —

against — silence and dirt

& hail bites

time passes, strangers alert

to hot pants shot through

— Lusty lopers — abound

— Hump your lute-sacks of grainfed gains of ground!

— Wolf it free in epic epiphany —

Invocation

Black knight white horse motorcyclist loons*
Scintillated spectator swoons
— Boypoet kick-starts his eyes on

Bevies of drumfoot balloons
Barrages of bar-raging aeons of goons
No body but he relies on. . .

Bob Dylan on the Isle of Wight
Back home in Woodstock they raved all night
& all day too — nobody
but everyone
spies on

— As the show-off orangoutang press-ups at his stall
Alehouse rocking jailhouse squall
Goalie-panther bagatelle
–plonks
the ball

— The slippery ball up the dastardly hall
The walls of death the halls of fame
The quaking walls of the city's game

— And the Goalie —
chittering, juddering. . .
Cries Wolf — Howling Wolf — scapegoat shuddering wolf
— Hurls them — inspired automatons all
On attack — back
on the ball — Ho the pack!

And the unflagging spirit unfurls, well aware
Hot feet on the ground, cool heads in the air
— Bodyminds — shooting stars — scudding akimbo —

* — Tune of Dylan's 'It's Alright Ma, I'm only Bleeding'

Nodding it in — tiptongue timpanic tempo —
Budding ball-ballet peony prance* —
Buck-bladder welling ponytail trance —
Giddy fray of swift-glancing deft-stippled chance

* — Budding ball ballet prance may strike you as corny
As roses read or rose-gardens thorny
— But that's how it is in the shaggy dog story
Called good sportsmanship — weather'd heads get hoary

— A dirtier dog would get horny right now
— And give Up writing now — give it up like fighting
Forever and a flyting and a haiku by Mao
. . .Fuck it —

What? — Sever these sheets
for the sweets of a cow?

— And an unholy cow, at that? —
Over my dead body.
Under my old hat
— Aye — for that
— for the death of all foul†
I **would** quit the openair palais casement bowl:

But my muse keeps me toiling on higher than death
To Shakespearian breath
—toeheld with the owl
— Flitgunned at the goal —
Jump, Toad!
Burrow, Mole!
—Plus the Idol fact of millions watching
Switches off the dull urge to splurge and laze
In baby-love swimpillow fleshpot haze
With pleasure planes pinkly pornograph dozing
To tune in to over head space blast-reposing
To visionary planes — windswept joystick nosing —

Or that's how it seems — beating batwing beams
From the play of duality — to subtler quality
Becoming a single, realer reality
Than leisurely wheeler-&-dealers' jollity
— Flying Objects
— cry Shame —
Really playing the game
stakes the claim to galactic egality

† — See the last 5 lines on page 359 of the 'Afterwords' to Horovitz's Penguin anthology of the **Children of Albion,** 1969)

. . Muscle-mind cocked to mate's move the timeless law
To stay fabled, stoic, as of yore

. . .Yarrgh, Hurr — Illuminations remain
— Electricly
Every-Ready (sparkling
Stone-plugged refrain
— For Satisfaction's action (& the stones remain —

For boldest pantaloon tight-thightrussed balling
— The dashing fury signals calling
Yokels from yodelling to line up before falling
in love again on the virgin terrain
Hear this my call — to hunt, and wind the trail on
— Uncover at a pounce game-traces since gone

— To wail **out** from the jailing oneway wall
For freedom
— freedom and love is the call
. . .Bird trills, far-flung formation swills
Till the ref calls a halt to interlock'd blow
For cathartic blow unto deadlock
kills — last hope

Detonating — simmering aft the hiss
Deploring some blotch-botched wideopen miss

. . .Celebrating the WOW — barking bogfight aglow
in local collective zen knowhow —
Footloose — tranquil truce —

treatied team-mates all:

— Yes — All sing High Table — all having the ball
— Everyman in league — sing beerhall balladeer
— Table-stopping hopscopping community siege
In good liege of highspirited empathy cheer

Swapping phrases, passes — real real-exchange
Here — where men as castles, and mountains, range
— All for One- One for All — Double You — tribal love —
Friend duende-duelling flungdung glove —

Having to shoot on the brink — **and** think

In trade wtih pub-publics that right loud enow
Parade own-grown foresights — shelling POW, telling NOW
— PUDDINGS and BOUNCE IT and — TRASH — and — OH **NO!**

. . .Yes, despite the leonine universe roar
Tender night rushes foam — Swaqkh, the wanderers roam
Roaring waves — most moodiest of militant loam
Rushing glory gloam out of lairy gloom
& zooming — pitch'd forward, and black — & through
— Blued at New Brighton — unglued from Huyton
Wilson comes back, child-starred Wizard him lighten*
To naked unpolitic open arena

(Athletics telescope cheat-proof demeanour

— No holds barred, spinal spiralling
— hardest of hard:

Lord, unsully mine ilps
To gush forth game praise
— Lead, O Ancient Feet
From these Antic
& lecherous lays

* — in deference not only to Captain Harold, but also to 'HAS WILSON COME BACK' — the saga of Wilson the polymath athlete in the *Wizard* comic, continued throughout the late '40s.

The Game

. . .to the epicure stillness, stadium hush
that succeeds the dying-down drone of corpse crush
. . .Mush of ticket-touts, cub reporters, wolf-scouts
Barkers, unofficial programme louts —
Ice-cream men, hot dogs, oompah bandolineers
Motley tipsters, majorettes, gawky- gracious peers

— Solempne procession of crimsonbraid strumpteters
— Battallions of Thousands Abide with Thee
— Thousands on thousands insatiate embattled
On all sides, brightscarved, riddling berattled
Air thick inlaid with pomp of parade
— Cameradoes connected in voice invoke
Insistent, exhorting — ill augurs, go broke!
— Strike up, kick off, wax fertile Glad Band
— Hoarse blurts, nameless contact in Oneness, ground

United through instincts closer than fog
(That caps the scene to
dim dome of a gasworks
– as seen from the wide berth of distant skyplanes.
Radio plugs in and the telly explains
But it's *in*side you feel the irresistible tide
Breaking wave over wave)
as side by side
Onward the regnant rockers ride,
Sweep the field and subside a whole township's plush pride
Like some pregnant phalanx- unbridled steed bride
– Delivered, relaxed – gunpowder contracting –
Apocalypse blurt
of prescient tense heap'd-up anticipation
– One foot put wrong may mean relegation
– OUR MAN'S HURT – bites the dirt – dread desolate cries

— Reserves cringe and tremble

— to quit conturbation

Step in dauntless

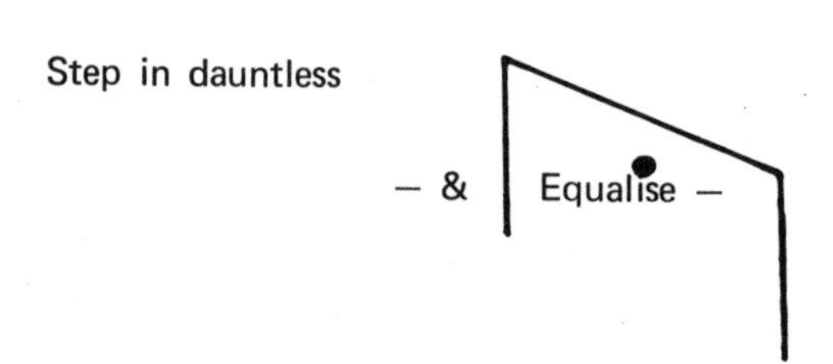

— & Equalise —

Let the news spread wiresped jubilant host

Stop-press amplified coast to coast –
We're ahead, We're the most – Allelluia Halloo
In unison Yoicks Huzza-yawp WE'RE THE WOLVES –

– Steeples of choirs people Goodyear tyres,
Chubb's safety-locks & the Willenhall stocks
As Walsall-ball tunes vamp Wulfrunian runes

. . .Wondering ear-views, Wolverine beer blues
Wulvering Heights, Villa-woof delights
Turn again to regain – London's Orient well met
– Nor let me forget, at Hampton yet:

Many the Hamptons drawn to play

– Hampton Wick – perfum'd garden,
Northampton Southampton Hampton-in-Arden

— Lionel Hampton — Hampton Court — great Littlehampton
Big **T**eaming Hampton Agonistés — Wolves
— Ye Pimpernel Pack Ye Glee
— Swiftshuffling past bottomrung'd Hammers v. Pompey,
Trampoleaning the ladder the decks and the docks
Husky- galloping flashmolten socks

— Atalán-
ticking over

ballcrazed

hoof- humdingers

— Jets of Mullen-skrim, Jumping Jim — Finney

— Phantastickal wingers —

Jaggery shaggery Symphony Sid

— Sped by Billy Wright

— the Gridiron Sidespin Kid —

Billy

— knight errant of 'might for right' —

Wirehaired campaign-brain Vikingshock Header —

Albion's All-time good bloke Leader

*Un*perfidious — terrier

stormtrooping bleeder. . .

Later, cuplinked laurel-balded goal-chain'd O'points meant

He won —

the hot seat at Highbury

— Order of Boot worth well mikel a ton!

Cherouted auld wolfery,

Toasting his pals with that skill-bruited loot

— Open-hampering hampers of bootfruit lopp'd full

From stalwart plum orchards ripe seasons topped

. . .Greyhound-spawned Wemblylawn'd mummer's memory sufficed

(Tho **juiced** in his gorrillorialisted cups) to store

A new pack with devises of wolflore galore

begaurrrh

— Stern conclaves — Venerable veteran coach

In holly and ivy league with trainers

. . .After workouts the lads lay massaged, footsore —

Warmed by his pep stalks of sage, hard-won wage

& steaming world onion-bowl gallumphing glaze

— as qwhan, a mere Whelp, a pup —

Tup-kinzossled how He, Ironwrought skip

Angelically bootskulled that entire '51 Eleven-ship

to League-*And*-Cup's top-tip — All Heaven's trip —

. . .But for the Arsenal's tried, & justly famed
Reserve of hothouse power:
No wenlock of wasps zap-suction'd that flower
– Turreted amphitheatric brawn-mower

In fumy face of which Whirr-wolves abandoned grope
. . .Tho every match struck spurr'd afresh
the Challenge –
To light up – flash out momently each half the finest hour
– What use, against our red & white-hot shower! –
Come throstle drops or shine, aye – whate'er the sky
– Outshimmering turnstile-riot storm's eye

Whether ball-love hove leather-enginedrawn
By mute and glory-be namelost pawn
– Or juttingjawed thrusty ruggerbugger Punchkonk
Rolls Razorsharp- shooter – Ronnie Rooke! – Or swart
'Bighead' Compton – Indestructible custodian
Of the Penalty Area Fortress – whose bell-clear kick
Would fairground-hammer clang his brother Denis off
Ball battening a crazy cricket-neck line
to the cornerflag
Thereat to pull his left leg back,
& Slice the leather orb
– Whizzing up and – split-

-secondly stock still
At the dead shed centre of the goalmouth
(just south of
the totterers
— For Doug Lishman's bonce to bounce it deftly d
Athwart their 'keeper's
o
despairing
w
muzzlehanded
n
dive —

. . .Dream-machine of a team —
Each man a Genius, each content — for
"Modest in Victory, Cheerful in Defeat" —
to be obscene — to be Seen I mean
— a small but gaily gleaming cog

Even where, in wet or midwinter season
The bed lay rampled to a murky bog

— Or frosted over — hard as glacier-ramparts —
They'd brace themselves,
Wolf Mannioned as the Nordic Middlesburghers,
In most likewise hard and strongboned harmony —
Erect through storm,
and failure of omened truth-to-form
— Like as if they were
Not London's gunmen grappling wild-wolves
— Not eleven men at all
But co-ordinated limbs of One Man
Labouring as 'twere
in every prime of Wife.

PETE
MORGAN

The Fame

Those **were** the daze my friend,
Those Saturn-deserted Saturdays
– The pitch glimmer'd as from the gladiatorpit
Loped out – THE Team, pumping Highland reels for cold
– Primed with lubricants, jocks, pads, embro-yo GoGo
& gristle-tingling exercises through the week
As the warrior wolfmen, proud cubs of yestern sagas
Unshakeable in comradeship
by man gale monster God

– Me was you is or always **can** be a wolf
– A silent exile cunning wolfpard bard at work
& play – a sleazy teasing tacklejerk
Tomcatatonic, regal – palais-gliding groom of spring
– Do your tousle-heady thing
– like any Joe King on the lone left wing
Hogfoot- warming out of his sausage skin
– Sizzling in, all the way inside
The raucous right-half left fizzling fright
– The fazed right-back left outside all night
– Free King switching farther out, full flight
Way out – on the ball – his outright, undenied –
& back – round the left back, slamming through – **wham**
– Hitting post for fun to jab it in
Flash as junkie's stash on rebound Blam

. . .Schazam

– Like Jamie Logie, Arsenal's laird
Frae far fair free Airdree
– Hardy purpellmellnial
worry-harrier o' th' dales 'n straths:
Richt rockfute wel **he** knew to trapbabble a mudsmear trick
Undared by any other dribble makár
– not nan oother sckribbled lines
meant sae swiftsinctly as Stan Mathews ever guid

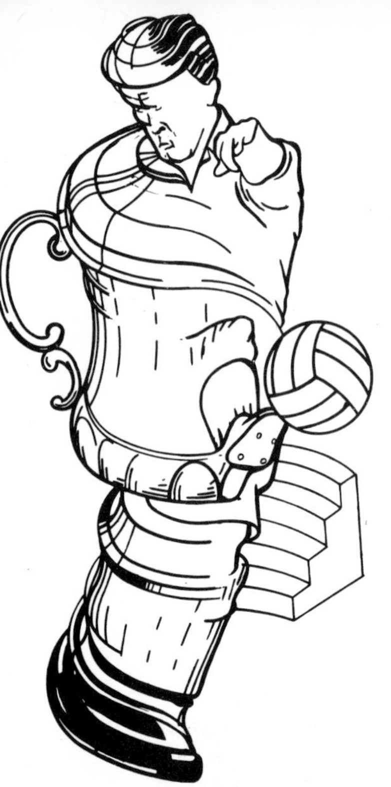

Like. . .

Fearless freebooter Freddy Cox

Infused from Hotspurs tore

Pole-vaultgleaping the divisions

to Trueformly score

The semifinal-splurter 'gainst his old club — placed

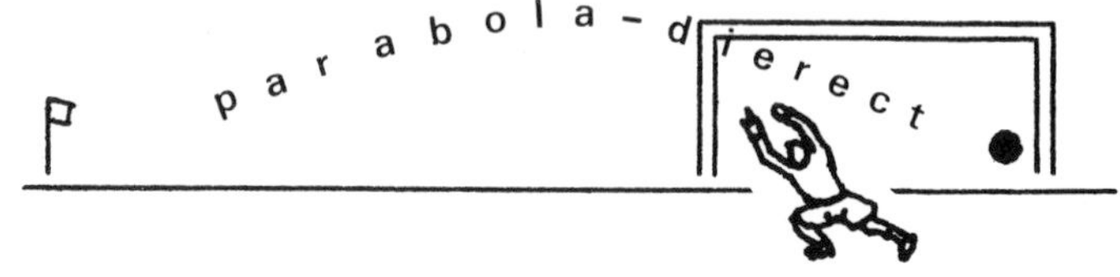

From corner kick

the last mid-second of thrillpackt extratime

Of third phantabulous replay

— Grassblade Jubilee!   Winnegan. . .   Toggers — be gay
— Look a header or frink back Mac
To (Nelson) Eddie — 'Football is my Business' — Hapgood,
Resorting eft to Thee, Dark Ages of Soccer
— Jocund plashing popyule airs
In City dells; and —
haunting the fell
— Grendel — the critic
Starved of the bells. . .

Till — "Zowie that dad
could drop lob-licks
in any goal area within
fluegelhorning distance"

Eddie Hapgood kept Leslie Compton out of Arsenal's left back position for a long time. Here Hapgood, clearing a ball, appears to have hoisted up Peter Buchanan of Chelsea as well.

— At such a stance
— Foxtrottoired internal
toetapt swervespan grime
The thrill fraught hill fought
Ball is never over
. . .whilst the sound of natives
applauding their brave
brigades — be they raiders
or mettle-helm home guard retainers

— Resolute, stoke your stoves
Rave, rove your ways
Throw on — tussle
hearty for your droves, fighter coves —

Rattle-swingeing flowers of friends
Lattice the terraced bawly hue. . .   Tho dusk
& dust & roistering rust descend —
Tho the final whistle scream finis against
The firmity of tribes' blast-custom'd noise
— In despite of pools mounted ploys police hoi-palois
Opposition buoys Every town up for the Cup
Whose sluice- juice joys on 'mid cascades of song,
Rains on walrusthick ox-heads of weather'd skin
— Ton-up kids flare the heart of Midlothian's wrath
With a charge that rampages the Queen of the South —
Lo. . .   Mrs. 'Alls toffee balls and the rest —
Best hopes
. . .of redblue evening suncat calls
Chorussing —
Waughaaaughaarrrraaaahhh — HuuuuuuuuurrryyyuurryyyeeeeaaaaaiiiiischW· · ·
— O lamby vocables!   Clomping delightfoot herds —
Scowl-yowling hotshot stars of Stafford
— Comets of Bromwich peerless Albion Aston Park
Belle-Vueramp lace enribbon'd biledrivers steer
Sheffield Wednesday thinking it's Thursday
Shops close early — midweek Derby —
Chelsea girl- guards guide pensioners at Leeds
Drinking in — the salt tiers of Grimsby — Mancunian meads —
Newcastle Browns through the loverpool'd towns
Frolicky footing feeds fried Eggman Saturday
— Arcbright acrobátwing'd lakenight ritual,
Our men and Their men —
perpetual victual —
Toptable Liverbirds watch out
— the wild wights are coming
— Glorio Glorio irate Borneo men
Put the wind up yon Ackademichal glen
— Stoke fumes throttle the Mill-walled Lions' Den
— Hibernian Celtic Rangers Moscow Dynamoes Ancient World
Cup Conquerors of Aurora
Proudfoot Boérialis floes are breaking- ice burning
Bush telegraphs of first-rumour'd scores
Of 2nd-half's endgames ultima twining
On and up and down and out-

door stagsole ballroom round & round
The land we go, Galahadding gumption's grail
— Moonbeam mist o' knights in due order again —
Mantic rituals done — clarion pipes, pirouéttes,
Pike- conjuring Klondyke goal-striker Debretts
— Eaglet agog to renew the fray
And assuage each ray to its shard. . .

Swooning silhouettes
Of shadowflit figures — trothplight chargers
— Broad awaking — playing
Football — pylon-sphere peers of
Spartan snowcape — human lightships
. . . Playing by
fusion of
feeling only

Since they too
are in the dark
of th' eternal sleep
Of the smouldering grate
official British city nightscape
— Sensing one another — somewhere there
In the limegrit sanctum
of cogniscated fair-play air

. . .Whistle's shrill rewires from mud-baffled foundering
To Mid-On-searing fusilade — lungeing,
plungeing —
Nudgeing knee-motors revved up canónic —
fire stud-tacks —
"Make space", sound off — just three minutes to go —
Rockets whoosh, Ack-Acks flack, brazen bugles blow
— as of old—

Young lads pick up easy-beat rhythm'ning combos —
Syncopate terminus showman- shamanics
Panic-blasting the Other Side's defense manoeuvres

— Joint vision jolts slumpers to Superman- oeuvres
— Jerks lines laid low to attack in concert
— Swoop-swirl hurdlers build up the tantric troupe phallus

unshackles endurance of
keep- cage and Palace —

The plunder of Molineux
From way out
down under
Their very jocks
— Proud cocks
Of that selfsame wake pierc'd asunder
(Cork chastity belts
— Sweet Molly Bloom's bloomers —
Now rouze up eld lionsmanes conquester'd thunder:
JYRRDIDDLY, Gádlope — Ja Heidi Y' hip. . .
Lily-whites gone to earth
— Frilly pants round grunt's girth —
Fly up at the onslaught — madcap forward-lines' mirth
Unwrapping net-stocking nest-keepers caught napping —
Shafting their balls' hasp home to the hilt

. . .Hip-hilarious lilt of total belief —
Crow brief, mangled chief —
Dazzling play of team's wit
it is wins the day
Squeezing out the good shout that fires hopes to a rout
. . .Out and about and with all lamb-blast's might
Y'HOP 'N Y' SCOP an' y crowd pops amok
to bursting bebop blockade rock

- O SOCK IT TO US —

Magi- wonderous flock

O yeh see the way they —
Effortless pillage the scenes —
Battlestarred rednose hephelumping bean—
Frogtoed tracktense starter-blockspit spleen
As of Blitzkrieg compositored by Brahms and Grieg — Hell -
It is true what they said about Dixie Dean —
Six-footer Mix-shooter rustling the sheen
And hurly burly laugh-butt Don Roper
— Bustle-throttling crowdbeck forward
—and-back bird
Whose pluck stonewalling Mathews had to be seen
— And Sir Alf, in his prime — whooo, cleared miracles
& blurred — the paths of Titans — & scores unheard
the like of since

— Chelsea's suave straight-up-the-middle elder
Centre-sprinting goalbuster Lawton

– And "Lino" Campbell – nicknam'd that
'cos he always used to rally & then fall flat:

Bobby Charlton Athletic Best
Boggled Blanchflowers
Lofthouse never missed
. . .But for life-jacket fistwaver Swindin Ted —
Grave Ring Road Raver — Brylcreem'd Saviour
— His one-arm'd catch swiftly check'd limbo's latch
& in-an-instant-flip rip-rap rear'd it to chuck
— So fluorvescently axle-grease plaid for time
— Saved the day clockwork-regular, cleaned the clime —
Bounce-rapelly clearances' straight-talking wand
Would scheme-send our Gunnery to bust the last bonds
Past any known onslaught at footwork's fronds
. . .Wing-halves arabesqueing like unchain'd calves —
No beyonds to descry the flawless finesse
That postwar- lumpen legion labour'd
— Litesome Mercer, MacAulay — ice hockey sled-saber'd
Alec Forbes tyroo-oiling through
the Forest bulwarks — tyree-ooh
— One two — Evanescent, incessant
— tobogganing throug
The myriad motley Alexandra crew
— Good henchmen mustering man for man
To th' international golden- arrow'd van —

Ne'er forlorn
Whilst there be such as Thee
— Fancy free,
Excabbalistic See

— Gunners of Caldonja — stomping ram's horn-swelling
Battering stampedes of —
Wolves of Britannia —
Tiger Bay bóyos — Yeovil yobboes —
Lancastrian ladds an' Dub'lin dads
. . .Ché: OLÉ ! — Friendly foe'runners, stay —

Belov'd, be winners be champs be chimps
— Be hinds be apes bejabers.
— Be gruff
Empty Shoeoo, Trumping trough!
— Be mass-ag'd and sing out Gusty in the showers
Ye- hotted springbok baths
Ripple pink-limned glory afterplay — be grim
— GrimmlimBimm in forfending thy lay

— afore summer's release-O sport i' the hay
with chicks i' the willow
— mossy quim-clicking pillow,
oak-sported boater- ribboning billow
— perfect bluesky regatta soft-silken water

— Yet let
be brimtank'd with legend the rainspawn hours
— Till you is me — us is — Utopia —
O Powers — play still

Tell how it is — was
— & with Puck- luck yet will —
O son, O foot- fabled daughter.

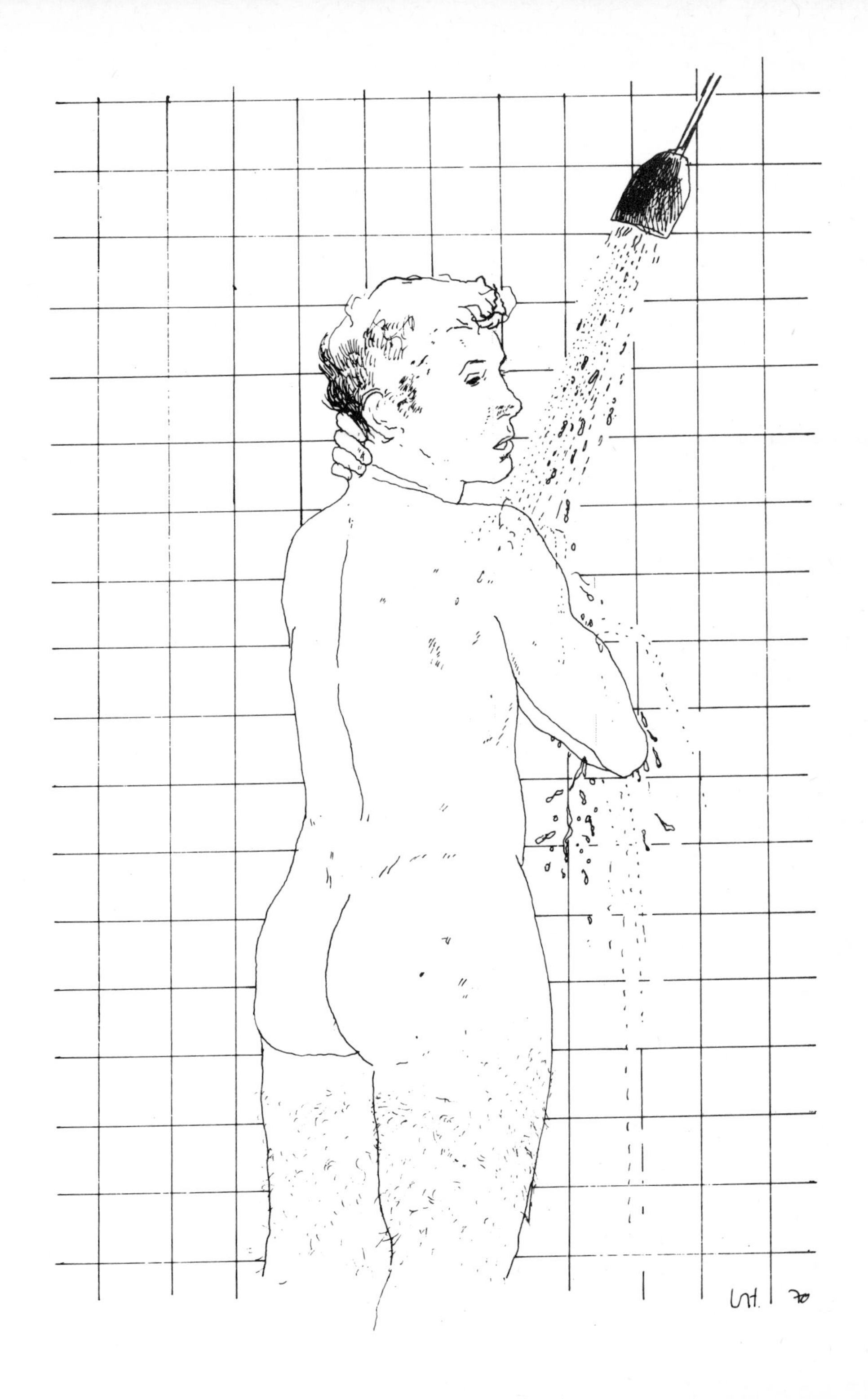

Half–Time

Tyger-tank'd with history
Supporters'
loyalties bicker
And drive on the energies
These moments flicker –

Yet the quickening sands give out
No more than the hour-glass counts. . .

No man grows wise without he have
His full times' share
Of winters on the field-run

. . .thus Sophocles.
But I double-dared
& spurned who Cared
– with Rimbaud glared
many an angry spell,
In blackest season played
cold rounds of hell –

Le loup criait sous les feuilles
En crachant les belles plumes
De son repas de volailles:
Comme lui je me consomme

. . .the wolf howls
the chicken squeals
– Wolf spits out the cock feathers
– Short-lived fleshmeat deals
– Like him – like the broiler
Word burns
– hunger turns
– slowly, stately
Wears out ye leathers.
Burns
Out with the bane

Yet – we polish shoes, tackle
The News
– & unhang the good boots once again –

And then. . .
Ice-floe cracking
— Knee-deep tapping

Avaricious, habit- humanised wolf
— Hang your head, your dream- lover
Snow White is dead
— Gone to her deathbed
All under the Chatterton
Grave wooden shed —

Long-drawn out foot notes
Tromp bone and knuckle

— Cheers chuckle, keels buckle
— & sink
. . .down to sorest shame —
conceding — Own Goal

— or Sent Off — vile
& verminous vole

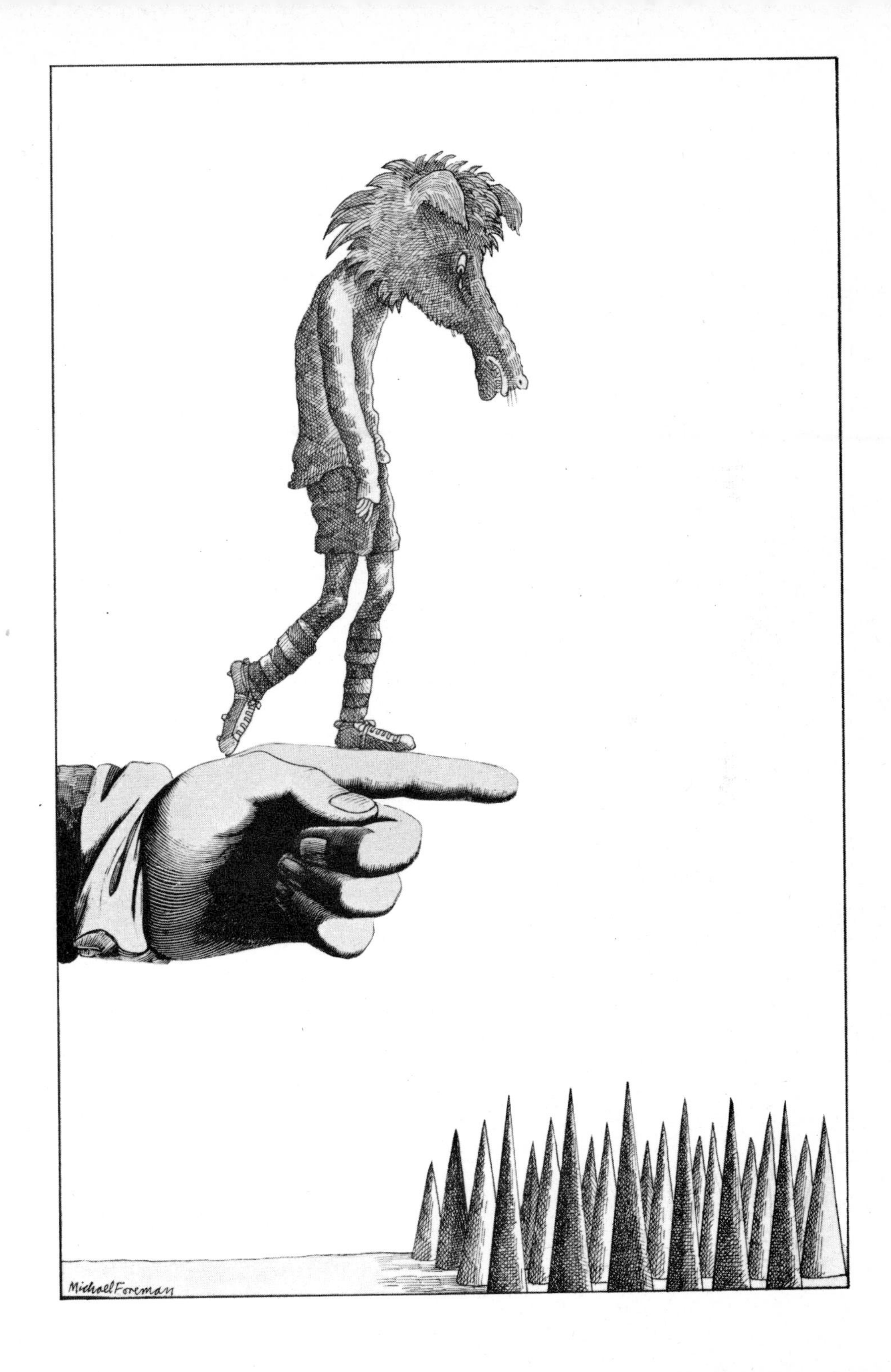
Michael Foreman

— for some unforgiveably fiendish foul
(albeit perpetrate
by A N Other)
— pronounce one Suspended

— what else but to howl —

— Branded Pariah, leper
— noisome
Befriender of fleas
— Leapless — that once proved o'erstepper
Of enemy athletes — cut off
— Locked out: hard cheese —

As search-patrols cordon release
So Hubris strips Jason of Fleece —

No peace — walled
Off — universally
Banished — scorned
Tho in more than a million
Fans' programmed hearts —
Mourned; at every heard blow
On the whistle — recalled

— to immanent
Redemption — privileged
Exemption
from the outhouse
— Unleashed
to some barely looked for tribunal's thaw
— Remission
of last season's merciless law —
Welcomed back
to the All Star-studded show

. . .to let go — let it
happen — leap
it aright — as snow
lifts a path
to all- oneness
. . .dear light
— pacified
. . . & poised
to fight —
Sack each site
through darkest frostblight —

. . .Erstwhile prodigies now bums are remember'd tho dumped –
Wolf buskers wool-ferrymen wolfwomb bearhug-slumped
At the footballen talus of Rock Candy Mountains
Where shamen meet thunder and spaceboats meander –
Striped windsock's tonic boon echoes delicate fountains
– Trippling padded Wuthering studied – promontories
prickly-hedge smooth/ sticky- budded
– Where Heathcliff and Wolfgang harmonise unmuddied
By conflicts or fear of ape chaos – hear
Wolf the herdsman, the healer, thief and smith
Wolfing soup and anvil, kin and kith
– Apassionelle criminal subdued by Sapphic
Plying lines of Time's beauty observed and classic
. . .Village headmen historic's archaic logic
Repels the invader – Robin Hood-feather'd hat tricks
. . .Sports messengers for kicks mix in blues licks
. . .Space-sages accord lords of life in mid-hoe
Flicking forth – and fifth goals to wipe out the foe

. . .Dream machine sent packing from bowling green
By Plymouth Argyle's treasure-chest expansions
. . .Sir Francis's team safeguards redbreast-blest mansions –
Armadaic home runs quell Charles Atlas-trained guns –
Drake's infantry drums beat a rat-a-tat woe
To the top-heavy weighted shoulder-to-shoulder
Attempts at rebuilding the smithereen'd boulder
That once was invincible – it's grown so much older
. . .Hear: Anglo-Saxonia – grant these scann'd notes permission
– 'tis to theee they look up, nigh sunken tradition
– thou: unbroken lion – holding mind's eye on
– mine cargo to Zion –
bereft of shipmates
– poop'd distance from Rome
– that foretold Ibn Ezra's long way home
via Battersea, Watling Street, Hadrian's sheaves
– lost to Seafarer, Wanderer – dovecoated eaves
where the marble still breathes

— no way out but for leaves — of frozen grass —
Pounded wailer's brass — trumpeting "Winter is
a-comin' in
— Loude sing Goddam"

— But householders dread nought
of worth's battering ram —

Arsenal newsmaker is seller of news

BIG MOMENT: Jimmy Logie shakes hands with Premier Winston Churchill before the 1952 Cup Final, which Arsenal lost to Newcastle, 1—0. In the centre, Joe Mercer.

ANOTHER PITCH — Logie, the newspaper vendor.
STANDARD PICTURE: FRANK TEWKESBURY.

NEWS ON CAMERA

ACTION MAN — the Arsenal star at the height of his playing career.

By JILL PALMER

A ONE-TIME ARSENAL and Scottish international footballer can now be found selling newspapers at Piccadilly Circus.

He is 51-year-old Jimmy Logie, the Scottish forward who was a star player in the Arsenal team of the 40's and 50's.

Jimmy joined Arsenal as a teenager in 1939 from a small Scottish junior club Lochore Welfare. He played at Wembley in the Cup Finals in 1950 and 1952, and left the famous London team in 1955 to join Southern League club Gravesend.

Since then he has owned a pub, been a steward in a night club, and now has a newspaper pitch in the heart of London's West End.

Now he lives with his brother in a flat off Hatton Garden, and "just manages to make a living."

He is sorely disillusioned with the football world and never watches the game nowadays. "In my day my highest wage was £15 a week with Arsenal," said Jimmy, who now suffers from bronchitis.

"I am very disillusioned with the whole game. Once you are past middle age, you are finished with no qualification to do anything else. It is not so bad nowadays, but I was not able to save a penny. I would not go back to football now as a coach or manager because there is too much aggravation."

Jimmy was the football hero of dozens of schoolboy fans and is still recognised and sometimes asked for his autograph. He has a 15-year-old son who is an ardent Tottenham supporter and, although he says that he regrets playing the game professionally, he does his best to encourage his son.

Safe in grub's cot
Lost to outsider's lot —

". . .Burgher knows not
what some perform
Where wandering them widest draweth"

". . .His is the path of exile
in no wise the twisted gold"

. . .nolonger sprite pup —
high- price favour'd
flop

"Alas the bright cup
"How that time has grown dark"

– Temps perdu –
Backflash routes
– Mouldered fruits –
Vanished view –
lost arc
– O the park
Where we all
Used to play
– Fall on grass
Ev'ry goddam
Mad dog day. . .

– Tomorrow
Wolf-pilgrim
growls and scowls
– Barred from church even
– yelps and yowls
– Church contemns instinct's grope
– Loose limbed animal lurch

Yet he bears back
faith –
The residue
truth of his search
– Draws on
his paws
Re-laying pieces
of master-work –

The Feedback

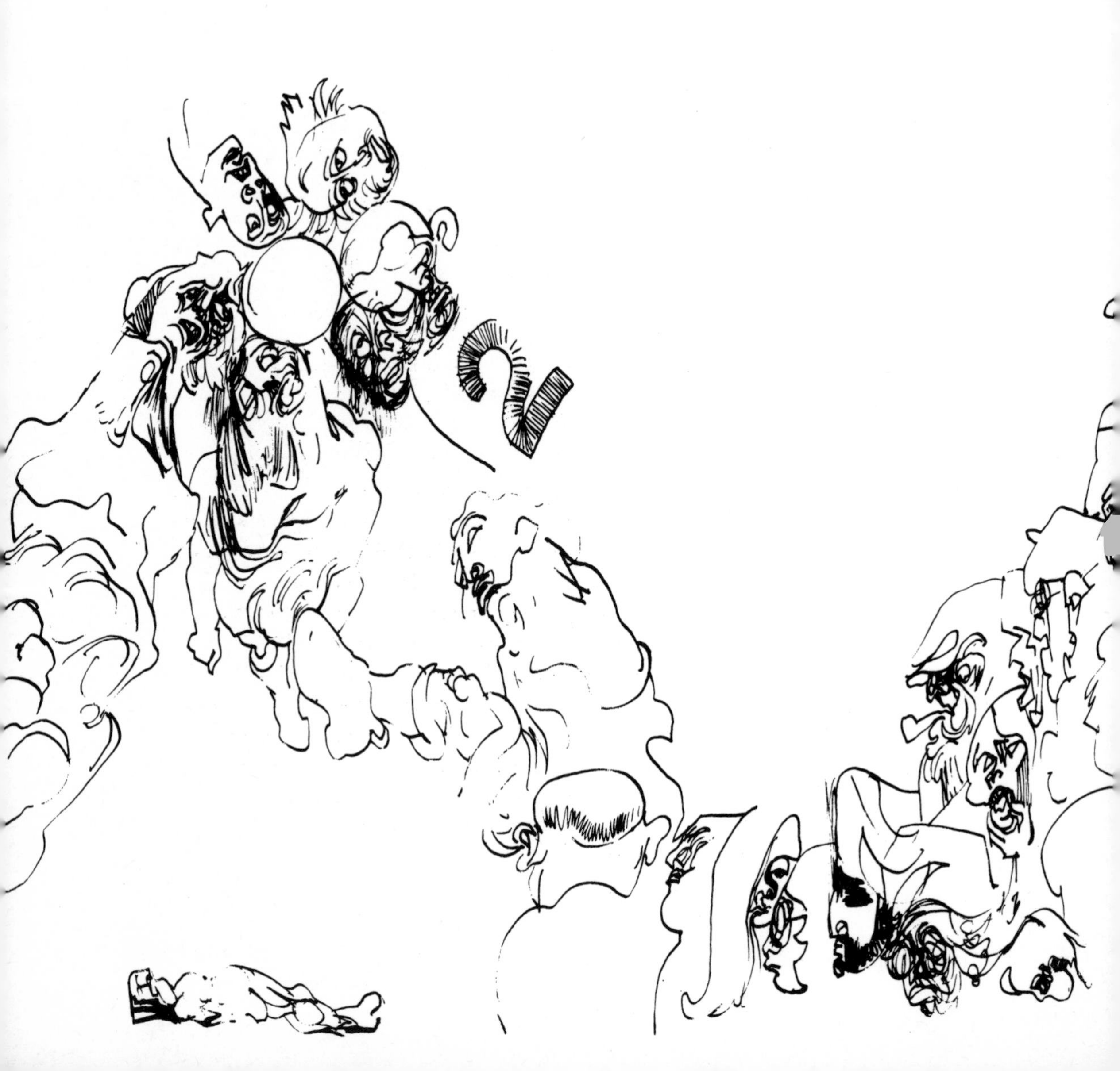

. . .And foul play flitted, for fortune
And fame
And the wrong man
full oft
takes the blame
– Yet – Sobeit
All in the same
Spirit of – heroism
& humanness betwined
– Rewind, play true
To your kind
Great game, ever shaking up afresh
The 'shook foil' beacons of Stratford and Warwick
– Mead of grass
leaves – roll'd sleeves

. . .Say, Bard
If Wolverhampton come
Can Brum be far behind?
– Aye, Be hinds
– Grind, titanic mills
– Make bread – shoot lead, frothbellying gazelles:
Be deers
Be drakes be
joying anteloping springing
Down the gully glide
up the field kick up
The Leek Hum the Heeb Glum the Deebfreed
Jostle-bristling newboys heave they hoes
Starting upstart steed-stoats shot from O' Groats –
Sere wandering to waste land's end forsook
– Bootled past the last Big Kick in the book
– Daily shimmy hoom huuooom, plimsole glimm
– Grurru-Om greeboom – bom bam Bim
Pinnacles 5 places O'er Prestone and Ham
Trasnporting cameras crane and zoom
– Right back bootlashes a quick mid-air splash
Stabbing limber the rollicking stallions rush
Manes fluttering
– wide lens rears up –
one more push

— Winnings reft from the crocodile jaws of doom

. . .And enlightenment beams through the conference room
At the perfect hug-bliss of each that conspir'd
To make the goal — jackpot circuit rewired
Safe as the house
— bumper din chomps the chimes

— But **after**

Jolly Good Fellows
— Late laughter done,
— Who cops for the vine,
— Merchant and Earl
Double- deal
What's left
— Lone werewolf slopes off

— Starvation line-goaded
— Gazes, eyes yellow

Gentlemens' Times
last swish of sable
the vaults and the girl?
— self-approbate punters
& desert the fable. . .
for the hunters?

from under the table
to gnash at his fellow
the vacant Dis-
exchequer'd arena

— Stuck at the seamy
Of cast off third-
— Rocked off his feet
— Clutches quiff
— By jackal-cops that sniff
— Them as dourly paces
— Keep 'the peace'
— Helm-capp'd keeper
— Keeps at bay, wards off
Every barely imagined
Will prove squarely invulnerable
As the Midland banks

cracked lower ladders
division stockings
by blacks & irish
at closing-time inspection
the Midlands' calm
the warring races
through all-night places
bankface balm
with his long fright- arm
windowcrash-&- grab,
to jailbreak McNab
to midland oilstoves

— No maidens over
— Go East from Midlands
— Fiddling griddled —
O Mercia, Mersey —
— Landed midland
— Grandly cloisters his coffer

for Bristol Rovers
cleft Casanovas
mercantiled Midlands —
for Mercy you cry?
proffers no reply
of mutton and rye

— Say goodbye —
Fight shy —

Because all they want & all you get
In the rainplain bleedin' midlands is
The flatlands
the mudlands
the ratlands —

— But for the vaunted

Glory of Sport   Olympic fort
— Vaulted turnstiles   yield place
— Gents and players   — all lovers
In accord   — the same race

As all loners   — hungry, blunted
Gun-runners   prowling apace
— Blinking ballboobs   in quest of the stores
Of a woodbin'd elf   a permpelted sylph
— No longer to wag   de-Plutoed at himself
On the shelf of the turfless

Regents Park lady grays

— Till no more lone   nor stray
Each new thing   free king's
Gorge-granted his say   abreast the downy roundelay

— For this, sweat caps — much thanks
— No more kneading dough off the trampslimed fingers
— No handball sneak- cajoleing fen-filthy fare,
Furtive-fearful each finn pfennig's chink chunky- there

Nor burying talons 'neath bushels of salons
At collosseum, college — "pursuit of the rare
. . .Big brass bedstead derriere —

The Work

Aye, when all doors be open
— Then. . . . . .

But now —
what of now?

We kick off anew
In Wolverhampton or Looe
— Blow a few minds — fall in love with
— Who. . .
Stroke hands will shake
"Have poet will wake
. . .Trans- fuse adrenalin
hot blue glands

— And bid spring fields adieu

Like the women & lads that ride away
— Soccer lords & cowbell boys of old
Slinging guns of wordhoard
— Shotsplat finsternis fold
Melting the gold
spiralling linkmen
— Stoking the hearth,
treadling the path
— Crazy- paving the way
— Parting the seas
Of time-overhonoured
Patriarchic gore

— Streak-lightening fox fizzling fur-red on the glades
— "Bare forked animal" but for Penguin's shades
— Passing over — carpeting the webb'd-foot floor
For wanderers
and wonders
to come
to score.

BANTAM CLASSIC

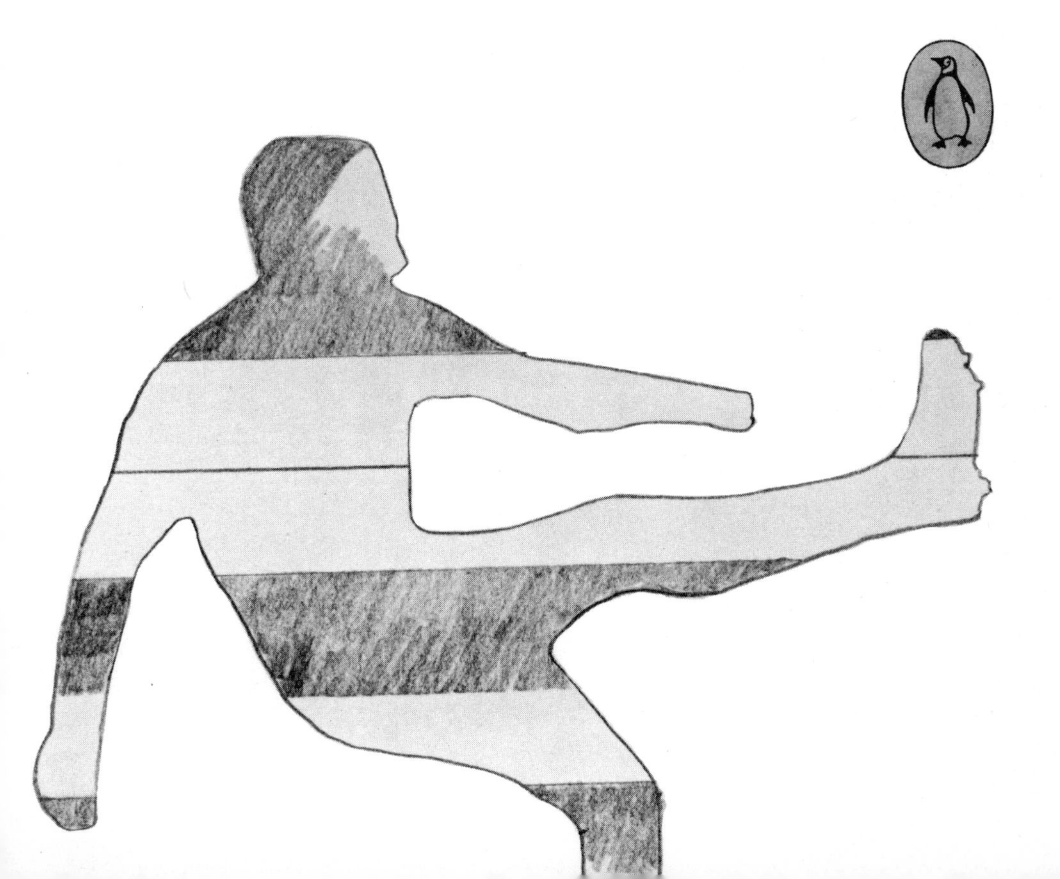

Wyrrd spak to my soul

'Beowulf'

— & i was:

With the Norseman swallow-titspat,

bared my literary loins —

With the Latin thrust for beggarwolves my coins

With the Romeman gan nomadic Commeddia

— Brigg'd flattbrogue pots of Básilic Northumbria

— Divined tortorella in pace dell' Umbria

— Sax- occult alluded — all players included

Caught in that eternal from muse- halls exuded,

Penned in language for fun till — wordweb finespun

Soared with Fainlit larkrocket heartburst —

Squawed with Francesca, quenched deep mating's thirst

— Anna does, Livia lives

— but Plurabelle's ring rang first

. . .Sang homage to Beatrice, Cressid and e'en Medéa
And the stream sprang not one owl's whit more the muddier
— I was a maze, I was a studier
It was a craze, it was
the brainbath plunge
Of life meaning art played by foot and ear,
Muscle and voice and tomorrow's yesteryear
Embracing the NOW without sorrow or fear —

Where Dylan Saint Thomas's fernhills annointed
Priests in Beat clothing Eleventh fingerpointed —
Our wolves 'terranean ash groves planted
— Lascivic gardens and astral domes
& rehashed Xanadu without retching for thrones
— It's the work the end of self-pitying tear
Outwitting false fear, rejoicing all clear
Mounting on to highest thinkfeeling peak
And there in stone infinitude carve
The unwritten rune of all time:
Rabbinic mantic medieval or greek
Careless of being considered a freak
Or a square or a pain in the neck of cropped hair
By societies based on same ties & shopped share
— Listen man,
Bird blew — we fly
Sing
dance
& cry — bits and pieces of high
— Sky and earth, fire and low
— Blow on
— I I I. . .
into You.

But poets were few
& even now all they say in most guildhalls
is — Balls
. . .If you shake it up
It's back to the walls

Extra–Time

— Staggering, marked, hired, tired
In the Midlands I did see
Musty lawns Bovis shoptowers
Pubs panell'd flesh-chrome plastic flowers

— Green enamel and diesel corporation buses
Murkily mawkish muttering masses,
Sharp- practising business bullies and asses —
Benignly genial turbanned indians
Semi-integrate bettingshops, back-lane slops
Outgoing bindustry incoming crops

— Till a sodden sudden essence of shape loomed
— An old old lady sitting- dripping
Drying out from the heavy small-hourly rain
Crouched like a towelstand
— Huddled stench in the corner
Of a bridge stair landing
— Dark person-ark
Back of New Street sterilised station
Sleeping ston'd on her haunches
— Grime rag-coat loose spread
About her doubled-up
hoar- balding head
— Snoring, and wheezing
Piteously.
A rivulet of her pee
Emanated to me
& I winced
and bled to true soul —
"On no account wake her up —
She is maybe nothing
But a poor
forklesss
faultless
despised
dejected
Rejected
rotting
body —
But see, there she couches
— Her own threadbare defiantly squatting hive
— Adream, alive
— & to all wolfish motions
Oblivious and inviolate.

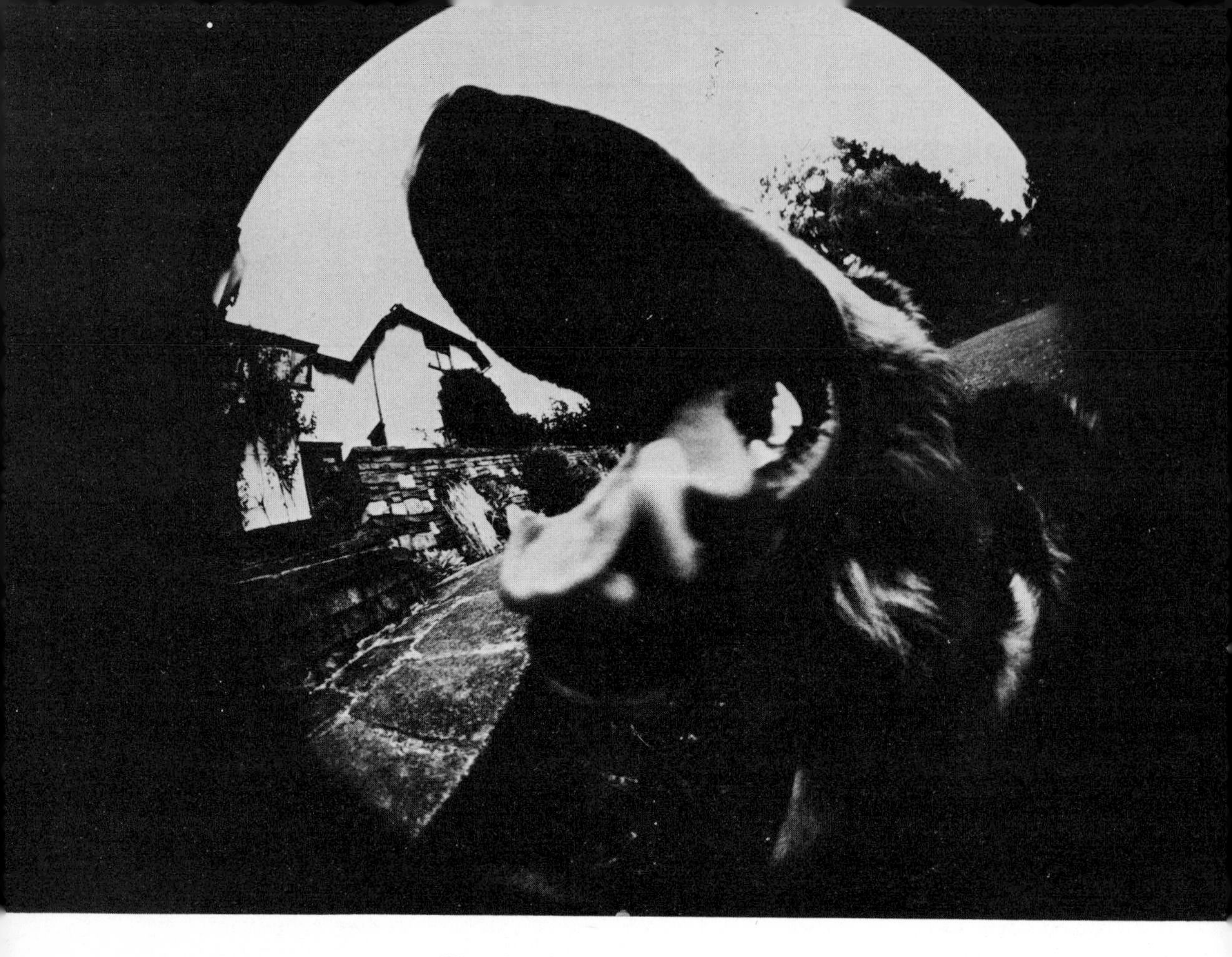

Then let the words tell
A true tale indeed:

Feckless wandering – blundering
One man band –
It's a hair-
of-the-dog-
that-bit-you's life
. . .Chewing, whining –
Waiting on and on,
Trained to beg
For scraps and a manager –
The carrion's castoffs
Slung askance for the stranger,
Muzzling his danger

— Thus it is for one
Who once — the lone ranger
Without a gun
— cocked his ear to the ground
To relay a new sound
Now bays
and wails
At the moon
In earnest of fun.

— Body's ache spews blood
Across the aisle unseen
By the official sinister
Representative minister
— Legal dock brief actor
Middle- classed rank and file
And snobbishly curtsey-smug certain smile
Of the bloodless lustreless fibreglass pile

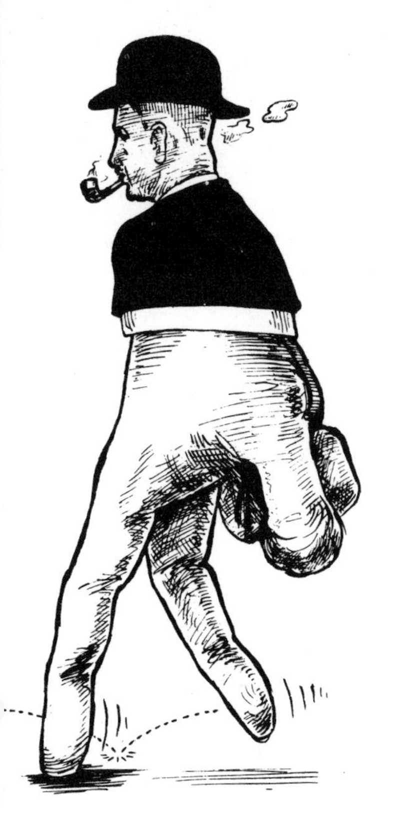

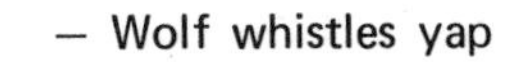

— Wolf whistles yap
— Spectral screetches from limbo
— Sick dog cringes
At the Master-
Director's tick
& tags at his fat wallet-
wadded bulge;
Leaks frantic
gutbuckets — scuttling
for readmission — Ta-ra tourney's troll-kinglit
Keepsake stronghold
— But his pass-out's too old
— Out of date:
no gold, no glee now

Tho he — old crock — just dimly remembers
how. . .once he was cock —
. . .Once. . .once — marvellous hack
He wandered and ran. . .hottest gun in The Pack

— The spick and span
— The wonderful Wolves
Wearing braised black-&-tan
— The wolviest wool
Vests in the west
— How they breath'd so deep,
Scored and shored in their sleep —
How heave-hoed & in full force middenships' sweep
Manned and breasted their Sysiphan chest
— That's long- lost to dross
— Gold devalued to rust

— Their stone's done gone bust

. . .dust to dust

And will wolf howl and roar
Till all tyger-lambs quail
Or back to the way
Where no pack with thee wail
— No grog nor ancient mariner'd sail
But the paste of a sniv'lling
solipsistical snail

. . . Oh no, said some
& forswore the wrack
. . .Pickt up new cloth of gold,
Licked the brass- warm'd back —
Kicked the Dane-cold pack for a shack

And the lilies came tearing out —
The lilies — like double-greased fillies
— Like aerdale volvoes lap wingcheek
With whisht- petalling curlews of even

. . . Even so doth the lily-white might
Clamour soul's handclap and choir
As pentitentiary blocks holler
"Great balls of fire
" — THE RACIAL ROCK GETS HIGHER & HIGHER. . .

& the cricketing poethead did lift up his sledge
& toboggan all over the alps

& broke ice to well lilies by sunclad clover
& dóve to where battle's clean lost in the past

– The entire cobblers seen through at last
Boots hung up to dry
to the eye in the sky

– For one day of blight
– Fínále-
festal
night
The Wanderer must die

– Hang up his Ever
No more to fly.

Yet the cricket-buzzing head
Doth bespeak him from his bed
Of softdown feather-pillow extasies –

Belies his professor
ship-
burial
'neath unpressed galley sheets of his own
Heavy
Self-
hooded shame

– Yet townscries best news
Of all Holy Head Flame

– No woolpack now, no football –
Then:
the heckle-hump'd fossil throws up
His shaggy haggis of tones
Not yet played out to groans,
Nor computer'd to bleep
– Heft-hulking heap –

And — gutted and ghostly —
Eternally creep.

— Eheu, burnished fighter!
The cold war goes on
— & the hot wars go on
And the Ex- hotspur man without papers.

— And the cold jam-ragg'd tarts a-clacking curt cobbles
Lamenting lost bobbles or steel heel'd support
— No army, ponce — manager — fame that survives
Tromping highways and byways — cheat-ruined lives —
Bought and soiled out,
flailed and impaled
—Hailstoned beyond elegy
or Blues
Sung for Sweetheart or supper or late-night booze
— Beyond 'Long Life'
— 'Final Selection'
— Bonded Scout's Honour's dues. . .

Wake

So — King Learing no more
Mill-tonic saws
crying woe
In sparse first morning glory glow
at Victoria Parks & Newtown centres
— The wonderment — the tumult
Of wizardry constellations'
Strident backdrop lifts
Scudding dubbin'd
lobmob commotions
& craziest flights o'nights
Closes down.
No vibrant surround
Save the littered windfalls
Of sun's royal rays, byegone Derby Days'
Single-course meal ticket stubs:
— Brighton early radios 4 — breezie girlie sweeps her floor
— First noises of voices found scatter dewdrops
As sparrows twit and graze-hop the ground —
As charwomen clatter trundle-whimmering —
Shatter gone dreams
to milkfloats' cash-register tinkle

— Green-&-cream chugs alarm-cock'd corners on time
Tabling toast tea and post — & listless flee
To thy pen-pent lair chides the fun of the fare
— Now swim, or drown in your ink
Midland watchdog's scare
Barks off the visitant's
Vain wondering blink
— Vainly scratching night-angled
Troth-droppings of think
From the clotted dream-locks of weir- hair. . .

Pitche queered, bitch blear'd
— A vanishing Self —
No Hobbit — no elf
— Top Cat Ungeared. . .
"I stumbled
when I saw"

— Grew to man —
Wanted more —
Wander'd on
round the bend
to end mortal war

— puts a good citizen
Outside the Law.

A traveller
from an antique band
Switching back
at Time's tinkering wheels
Spelled Eden plain: hark the lark
– Stay alight – or sleep sound
Through the dark.
Who's who is not
What matters – what matters is not
Who are You, Who are We – what matters
Is not
status- orient priorities
Nor cleverness in gamesmanships, but Spirit
– What matters any of it the speech withheld
& spasm shock jam
Of knuckles trapped in cardoor slam –
Is Spirit

– Came the dawn, we'd all but got
The spinning axles of the cosmos by rote,
Primal galaxies regained at the glimpse of a stoat –
Hills at nightfall quiet forest sown wild oat

– & warmest, sharing his vatic lair,
a wolfpoet humming wireless cold night airs

– Came to see
– unfree
– Marksman is marked man,
Hare is hound
– hunter the hunted
– Hanged man the accuser,
Hero 'born loser'
& the beast, too – is beauty

– & it doesn't pay
to be duty free
. . .now on his own
all team-mates gone

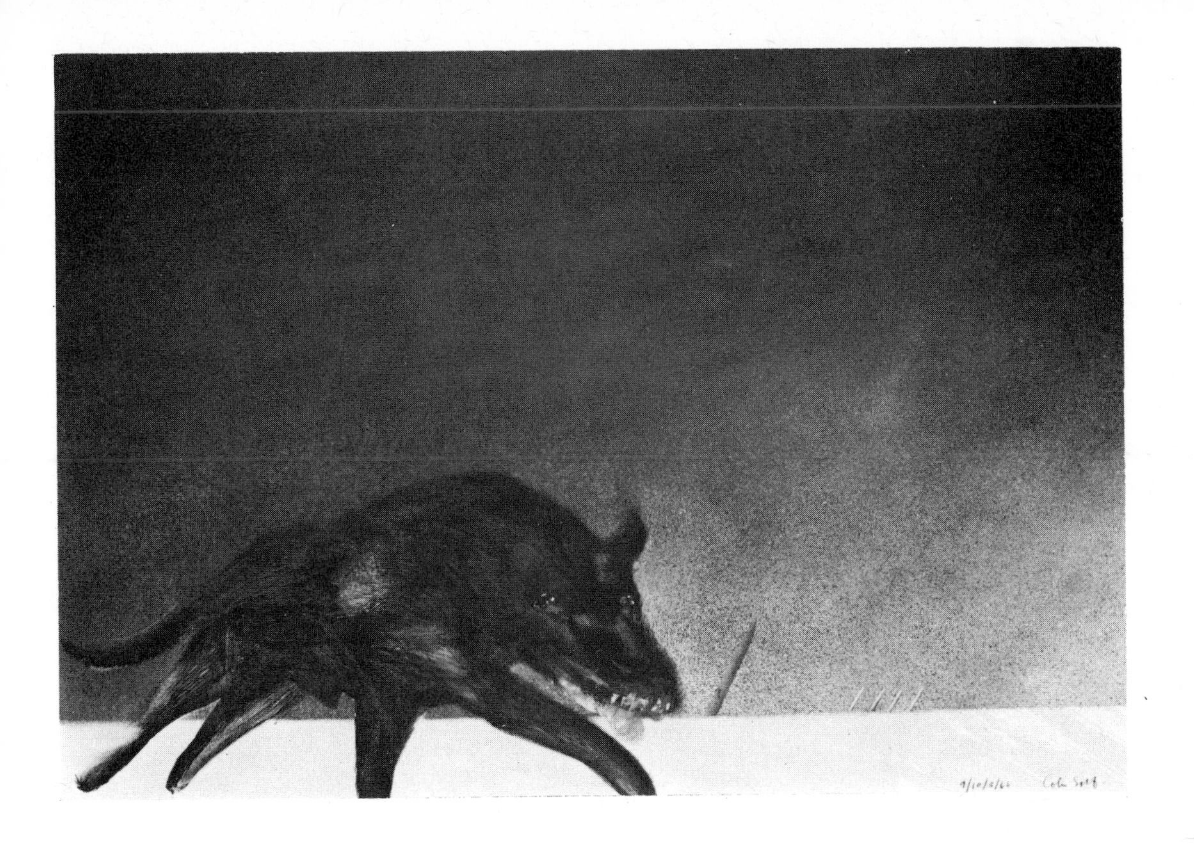

— Here Steppenwolf is —
Was — yes, today — still life
— Blue
turning
grey —
Black to
no play,
The fates seem to say —
Doomed. . .   Torn
Alien. . .   Forlorn
— Why were we born

. . .the doomed Midland Reds
the doomed Negroes
the doomed New Yorkers
& middleeuropeans
— all doomed

— & especially
the whites

— excepting — *no* body's white
— "Pinko-greys" by Huxley,
"Ofays" by "Spades"
— the whole stupid scene
of skin deep vision. . .

White
beard Sikhs
still smiling in
to eyes
— & I to theirs
On the rustle-bustling breakfisted main-street —
They're not late they're philosophic, sedate
Rippling Saharas auras tranquility —
Football? — Philtres oasés Poeises
Music — interpenetring entránceing dancing
Women — humbly beaming —
lightshow mosaic
Of gentle peace cloths
. . .It is said
Peace opens, war locks
— Yet these gleaming pearl teeth and saris
Stun labourers and stuffshirts to envy, then frenzy
— All 'Coloureds' not "ruddy" or friendly-servile
Resented — hated, as "fucking Jamaicans"
By greedneedy Rat- Powellhoused Native-citizens
Hard put to share rare IN-protectors —
& West Indians dig: B R I T I S H S T I N K
— Sad badmen of Birmingham City

. . .Who cheats at games, 'tis said
Cheats at life
— & most battlement-owners cheat.
I AM I AM Iambic lambs bleat,
Song's rangers rage
At givers of cups & rings profane
— in vain

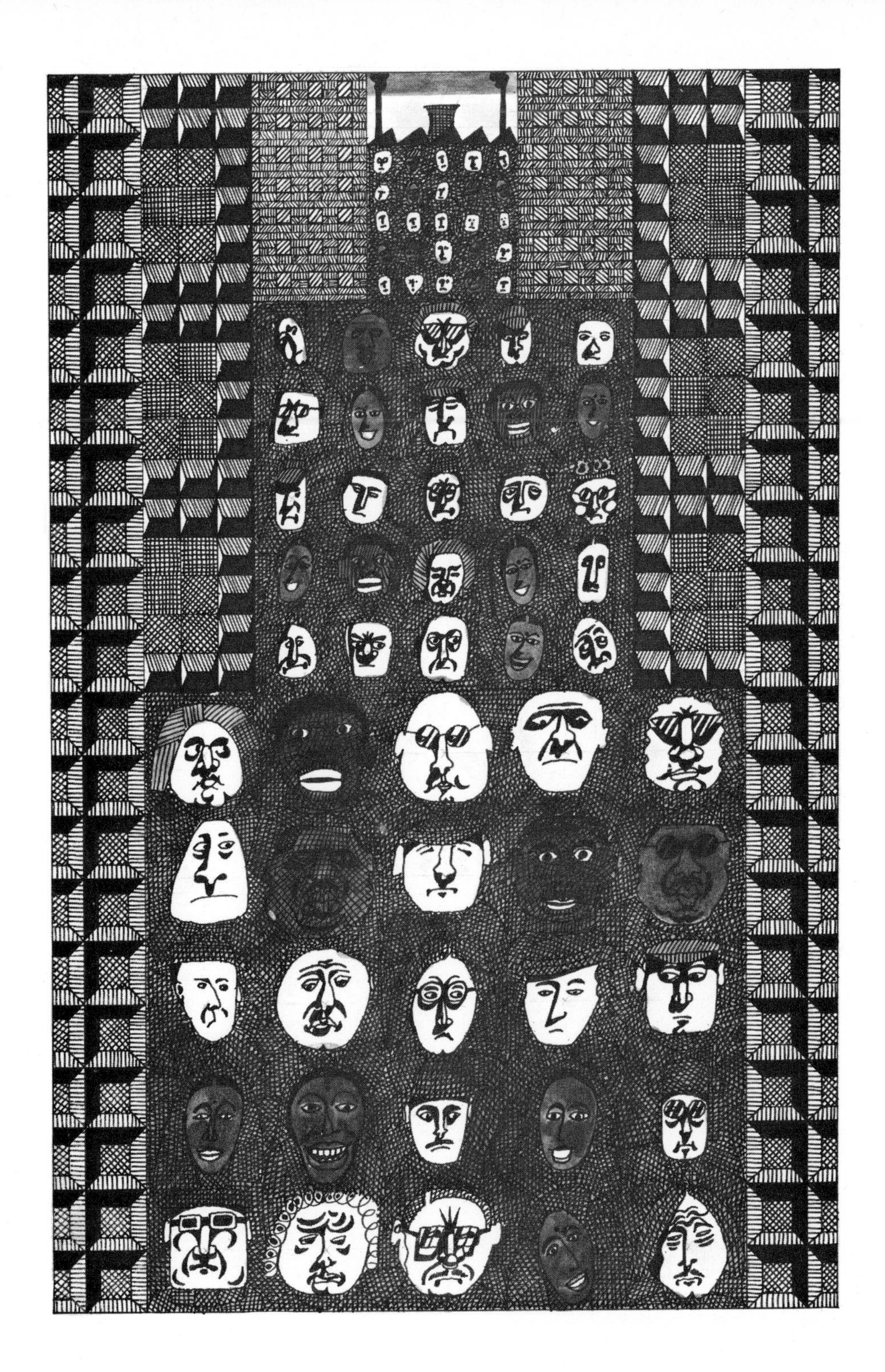

in vain
— All gone.
Wolfman's left
Alone to connect
— froze spuggie chirps
kennel'd hound burps
& jeers of the smear
gear another day
— a year
— 'rest of life'
without hay.
No cheerleader's lamp
now stirrups the stump
for his wandering on
to the dump afar hence
— where to flee wolf untaxed
sate state sanctuary
bona fide undenied
fulsome fortitude due
in some foreign fastness
most lauded bless-guest

As even now
— Tho accurs'd
The toothless untouchable wolves
& upholstered gunners of yore —
Veterans of the sporting life
The slag pits and junk quarries,
Stale meat-trucks and distance lorries
Old taxis throb, hobs hurtle on
Running the roads for a pricelss prize
Or broken back — for Tantalus's rise —
To be probably smashed by Damocles, good guvnor —
Smashed on the altar of sale-soldier'd Southerner

— Position magicians — toil on,
oil your hubs
— Scout — cubs — aery vapour rubs
To local habitations
— let the masses hear
Tho old crowds be gone
Forever — over to Bingo
— Squeeze out the orange,
Sprinkle the rind — even sightless,
Out of mind

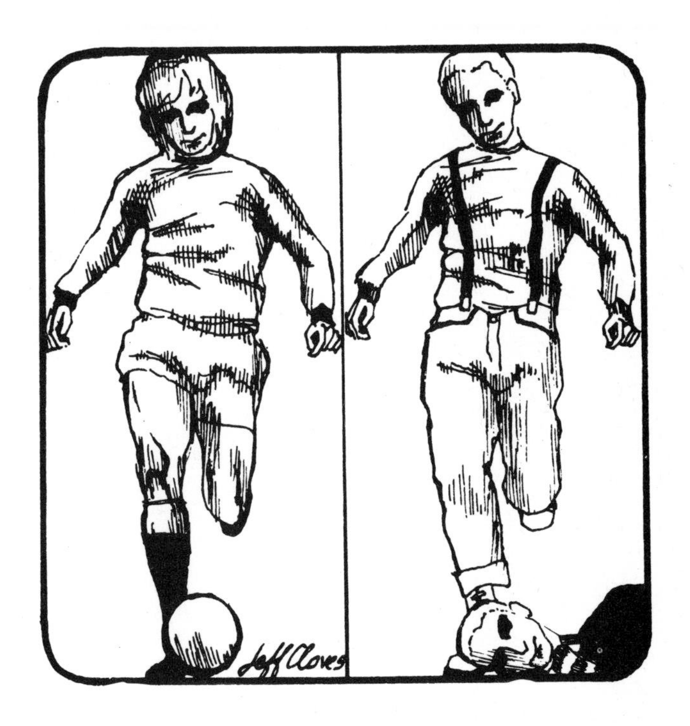

— Sing on, ever on —
Beyond — no aside —
Loss of cup — of country,
continent — universe —
Even unto —
sewers of blood
— Tho they put the boot in
sewers of blood:

— Singing blood on the hands of hate
Streams out — must outrun
the stamp-out of hate

— To break out — flout aloft
& beat the flood,
lie down with the musk-ox

& rise with the day
— kick off again
on the unspoken road,
cross fields anew
— to renew and remind
the chanticleer go-round

as songbirds of mirth
come out on earth
& do
what must
be done
as they say
it is
in heaven —

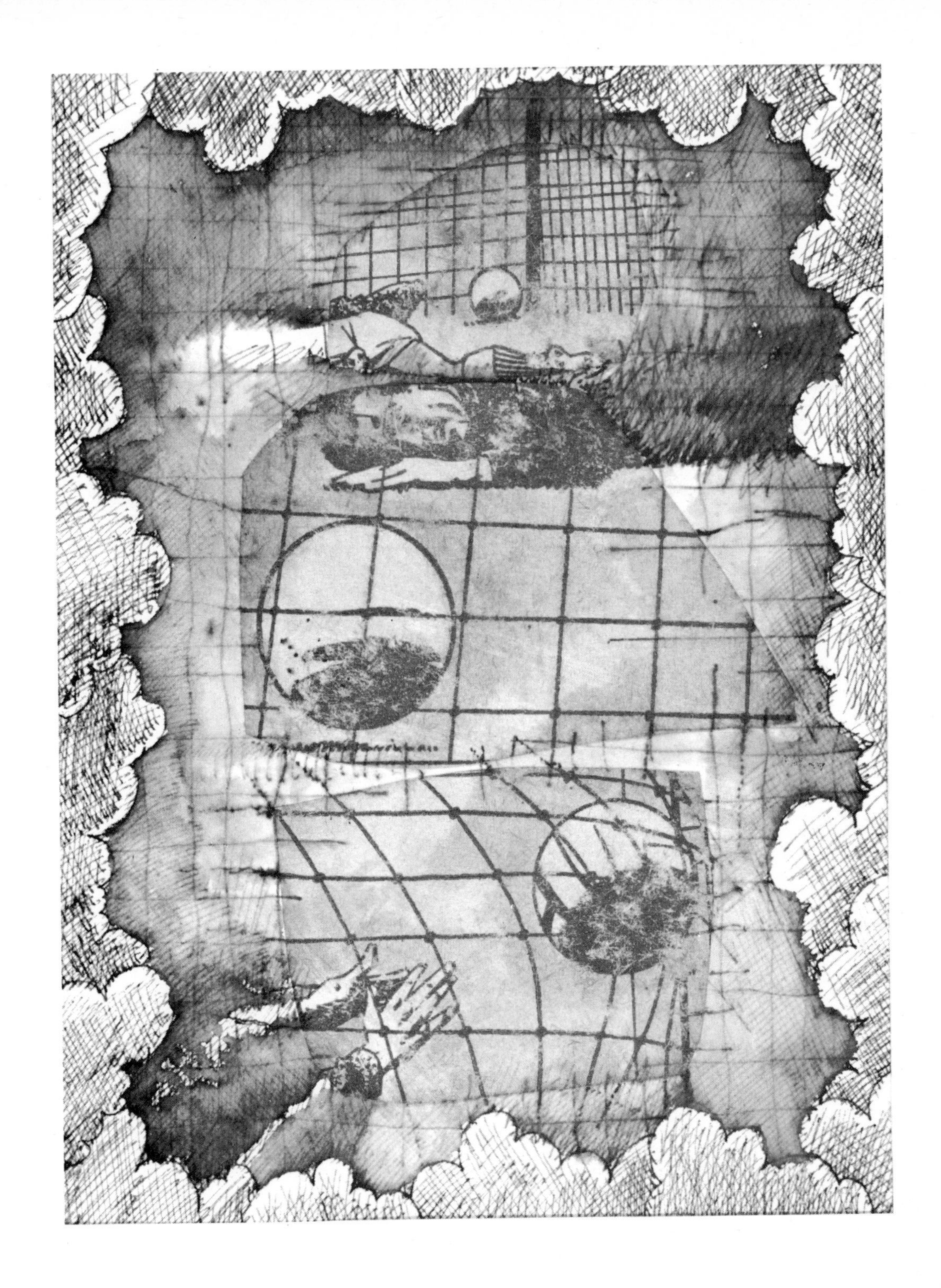

The Resurrection

Saved –
Skins peel, blood dries –
The Wanderer
of wolfdreams
lies dead.
Belly of Lead
dissolves in the void
– Lines of iron
and crags
Skip out of his head

– He rises again
like a thane
newly wed

– Opens the lightning-flash
soulbody mouth wide
for the other side
of the farther field
– shot over –
Far over
the first range of hills

Floats and flows
– delivered –
O winnowing rills
Of sacred rivers

– Eternal Life stills –

... and The Life

It was
— Let it be —
It is
The worry- quarried Wanderer:

He wondered
At Home

& wandered
away —

& recreated
— Back Home Again —
The Recollected Day

— Wolf-weary —
yet marvelling
each workaday play
— this moonlight final —
Wand's worth Assay

— Transplanted perennial —
Withdrawn from the Lists
Deep in love
High above
Maundy meat-market mists

. . .It is
The diehard
Homing Bard
— that rambled —
at home
— gives his best —
rumble- tumbled
away

— & rejoices —
Life's Cup
ancient youthful
feet up

— Full Grown —

for
The Great
Glad
Day